Author Fredrick Buechner describes *compassion* as feeling what it is like to live inside somebody else's skin. We move from empathy to compassion when we act on what we know. Kathy Perret and Kenny McKee provide pathways for understanding those we are coaching, as well as ourselves, and ways for taking action on what we know. As you read, you will reflect and plan—critical practices for coaches.

—Steve Barkley, coaching and leadership consultant, PLS3rdLearning, and author of *Instructional Coaching with the End in Mind* and *Quality Teaching in a Culture of Coaching*

Compassionate Coaching is one of those books I wish was available when I was a new coach. Kathy Perret and Kenny McKee carefully guide readers through a series of chapters designed to boost confidence and competence through some of the most challenging aspects of coaching. Armed with a GPS for coaching, readers will appreciate the real-life scenarios, practical advice, and tangible tools for doing this work. It's an indispensable tool for any instructional coaching toolkit.

—Stephanie Affinito, literacy teacher educator, author of *Literacy Coaching: Transforming Teaching and Learning with Digital Tools and Technology* and *Leading Literate Lives: Habits and Mindsets for Reimagining Classroom Practice*

Compassionate Coaching is like a warm blanket on a cold day, offering comfort and security. It uses real experiences to name and explain routine challenges that coaches face in schools, both their own professional challenges and those that teachers experience. After unpacking the challenges, Perret and McKee draw from their extensive experience as coaches and coach champions to offer time-tested techniques, tips, and tools to understand and address the challenges. This knowledge equips readers to coach with high levels of personal regard for teachers.

—Joellen Killion, senior advisor, Learning Forward

Instructional coaching is both rewarding and challenging. In *Compassionate Coaching*, Kathy Perret and Kenny McKee address some of the most difficult parts of coaching and help both new and experienced coaches understand how to effectively navigate through those areas. This book is both insightful and practical and will be a valuable reference for years to come.

—Sherry St. Clair, author of *Coaching Redefined: A Guide to Leading Meaningful Instructional Growth*

Compassionate Coaching provides a clear roadmap for navigating the barriers to instructional improvement teachers face. As former teachers and current coaches themselves, Kathy Perret and Kenny McKee identify and define six situationally based teaching barriers, offer coaches guiding questions for effective conversations, and outline planning tools and resources to move practice forward. Throughout the text, clear examples illustrate the barriers, and action-oriented professional learning (for both teachers and coaches) illuminate a way through. This is a book I will continue to refer to in my coaching work with both teachers and leaders.

—Allison Rodman, professional learning designer and facilitator, author of *Personalized Professional Learning: A Job-Embedded Pathway for Elevating Teacher Voice*

Compassionate Coaching

Kathy Perret • Kenny McKee

Compassionate Coaching

How to Help Educators Navigate Barriers to Professional Growth

ascd

Alexandria, Virginia USA

1703 N. Beauregard St. • Alexandria, VA 22311-1714 USA
Phone: 800-933-2723 or 703-578-9600 • Fax: 703-575-5400
Website: www.ascd.org • Email: member@ascd.org
Author guidelines: www.ascd.org/write

Ranjit Sidhu, *CEO & Executive Director;* Penny Reinart, *Chief Impact Officer;* Genny Ostertag, *Senior Director, Acquisitions and Editing;* Susan Hills, *Acquisitions Editor;* Julie Houtz, *Director, Book Editing;* Jamie Greene, *Editor;* Thomas Lytle, *Creative Director;* Donald Ely, *Art Director;* Georgia Park, *Senior Graphic Designer;* Valerie Younkin, *Senior Production Designer;* Kelly Marshall, *Production Manager;* Shajuan Martin, *E-Publishing Specialist;* Christopher Logan, *Senior Production Specialist*

All web links in this book are correct as of the publication date below but may have become inactive or otherwise modified since that time. If you notice a deactivated or changed link, please email books@ascd.org with the words "Link Update" in the subject line. In your message, please specify the web link, the book title, and the page number on which the link appears.

PAPERBACK ISBN: 978-1-4166-3020-3   ASCD product #121017   n6/21

PDF E-BOOK ISBN: 978-1-4166-3021-0; see Books in Print for other formats.

Quantity discounts are available: email programteam@ascd.org or call 800-933-2723, ext. 5773, or 703-575-5773. For desk copies, go to www.ascd.org/deskcopy.

Library of Congress Cataloging-in-Publication Data
Names: Perret, Kathy, author. | McKee, Kenny, author.
Title: Compassionate coaching : how to help educators navigate barriers to professional growth / Kathy Perret, Kenny McKee.
Description: Alexandria, VA: ASCD, 2021. | Includes bibliographical references and index.
Identifiers: LCCN 2021008218 (print) | LCCN 2021008219 (ebook) | ISBN 9781416630203 (paperback) | ISBN 9781416630210 (pdf)
Subjects: LCSH: Mentoring in education. | Teachers—Professional relationships.
Classification: LCC LB1731.4 .P47 2021 (print) | LCC LB1731.4 (ebook) | DDC 371.102--dc23
LC record available at https://lccn.loc.gov/2021008218
LC ebook record available at https://lccn.loc.gov/2021008219

30 29 28 27 26 25 24 23 22 21   2 3 4 5 6 7 8 9 10 11 12

*To the coaches in our own lives, formal and
informal, personal and professional, who supported
our growth in the ways that mattered, built our
confidence, and coached us with compassion.*

*To our families, friends, and colleagues who
listened, discussed, and took care of business while
we wrote, rewrote, and wrote even more.*

*To our #educoach buddies and our
amazing PLN for inspiring, teaching,
and pushing us to be better each day.*

*To you, the reader, who thought this
book could help your coaching journey,
we appreciate your support and look forward
to learning from you as we continue our
goal of #compassionatecoaching.*

Compassionate Coaching

How to Help Educators Navigate Barriers to Professional Growth

Foreword

Has there ever been a time with a greater need for compassionate coaching? As I write this, we have lived through more than a year of the COVID-19 pandemic, an event unlike any we've experienced in our lifetimes. People around the world are encountering difficulties that no one could ever have anticipated. Our family members, friends, and colleagues have seen their jobs turned upside down—if they still have jobs—or they watched helplessly as the pandemic had a devastating impact on the health of loved ones.

Coaches stand at the crossroads of all this change. They continue to do their best to support teachers who don't know what their jobs will look like from one week to the next. They work with teachers who are asked to teach online, then teach face-to-face, and then teach hybrid—and to do it all with applications they've never used before. I'm certain there are thousands of educators who would say they only survived the pandemic (professionally) because of the help of their coaches.

Coaches need to cram to learn all the new apps and strategies so they can support teachers. Carrying their own personal burdens, they must work with compassion when teachers have difficult moments. They must persist, even though they, too, don't know exactly what their job will entail or how it will change. They must show heroic compassion.

Now, thankfully, they have Kathy Perret and Kenny McKee's book, *Compassionate Coaching*, to help them do this extremely challenging work.

We can better understand the value of this book when we consider the unique work that coaches do. Coaches facilitate what I refer to as "inside out" professional development. Unlike "outside in" professional development—where leaders choose practices that teachers are expected to learn—"inside out" coaching begins with the real-life challenges teachers face. And that is precisely where this book is focused: the interior landscape of coaching.

Perret and McKee provide heaps of useful ideas coaches can use as they conduct "inside out" professional development with teachers. Specifically, the authors provide tools and knowledge coaches can use as they work with teachers who are experiencing a lack of confidence, failure, overload, or disruption. Perret and McKee also have suggestions for coaches who are partnering with teachers in challenging school cultures or who feel isolated. Truly, any coach will find something useful in the pages of this book.

The pandemic is temporary, but the human spirit is impossible to stop, and we will move on to face other challenges. In the meantime, we have *Compassionate Coaching* to help us get through. Then, when we are finally on the other side of COVID-19, we will have this book to help us address the new challenges that come our way.

Jim Knight
senior partner, Instructional Coaching Group

Introduction: Breaking Through

A substantial amount of research on coaching, both within the education world and outside of it, has been published over the last decade—so how to best coach teachers should be clear-cut at this point, right? Well, kind of. Although we know more than ever about how to make coaching programs successful, many educators still find the process to be harder than they'd imagined.

From our discussions with instructional coaches, teachers, and other school leaders, we've found that there are several common barriers to instructional improvement—and we have also seen how personalized coaching empowers teachers to navigate these barriers. In our experience, coaching with compassion and in a way tailored to the individual can result in transformational improvements to student achievement and teacher work satisfaction. In some cases, this kind of coaching can even shift the trajectory of whole schools.

Surmounting Barriers

Whether you are currently in a teaching role or not, if you're reading this book, you've probably had teaching experience. Think back on your students. Did any of them face barriers to learning? Perhaps you had a student who took on too many responsibilities and had trouble juggling them, so you helped him figure out a plan. Or maybe you had a new student who didn't know where she fit in, so you suggested some clubs she could join.

Most of the barriers you've helped students surmount have probably been related to the five core competencies identified by the Collaborative for Academic, Social, and Emotional Learning (CASEL): self-awareness, self-management, social awareness, relationship skills, and responsible decision making. By developing these competencies in children, we are able to address the needs of the whole child (Durlak, Weissberg, Dymnicki, Taylor, & Schellinger, 2011), but adults also need to develop these competencies—which is where instructional coaching can support teachers in navigating barriers.

Becoming a Coach

When you began coaching, you entered a new dimension of the school environment. Chances are you landed your new position due to your own skills and experiences in the classroom. Someone saw leadership characteristics in you, even if you yourself weren't aware of them. You were hired because of your unique qualities—your content expertise, perhaps, or your rapport with your peers, student achievement results, growth mindset, or a combination of these qualities and others.

We (Kathy and Kenny) both entered our coaching positions due to our content backgrounds. Kathy had a strong literacy background both as a classroom teacher and consultant; Kenny had studied and refined his classroom into a place for student-centered English language arts. With some help from instructional coaching literature, training, and input from other coaches on Twitter, we set out on a path of trial and error, with no choice but to get comfortable with figuring out our roles day to day.

You, too, probably entered your position with more questions than answers about instructional coaching. You've had to get comfortable with learning in the moment. In his book *The Learning Challenge* (2017), James Nottingham proposes that there are seven stages to what he calls the "Learning Pit": (1) pick a concept, (2) identify contradictions, (3) examine options, (4) strive for meaning, (5) connect and explain, (6) enjoy clarity, and (7) apply and relate. These stages can serve as a roadmap for coaches, both in working with teachers and for breaking through barriers we face in our own practice.

Compassionate Coaching

It is important to remember that barriers to effective teaching are neither permanent states nor character traits; rather, they are temporary challenges we can overcome with the right methods. In this book, we identify six common barriers teachers face and six corresponding practices for surmounting them, which we refer to as compassionate coaching focus areas (see Figure 0.1).

FIGURE 0.1

Teaching Barriers and Compassionate Coaching Focus Areas

Barrier	How It Feels	Compassionate Coaching Focus Area
Lack of Confidence	I don't have the skills to do my best work right now.	Partnership (Chapter 2)
Failure	I don't have the power to do my best work right now.	Empowerment (Chapter 3)
Overload	I don't have the time to do my best work right now.	Prioritization (Chapter 4)
Disruption	I don't have the processes to do my best work right now.	Routines (Chapter 5)
Isolation	I don't have the community to do my best work right now.	Connection (Chapter 6)
School Culture Challenges	I don't have the environment to do my best work right now.	Openness (Chapter 7)

Addressing Reluctant Teachers

A popular request on our #educoach Twitter chat is for insight on how to coach teachers who are resistant to the process of coaching. However, the more we discussed this topic, the more we realized that resistance is really just a symptom of greater underlying problems. If teachers appear reluctant to be coached, it's worth considering whether the issue lies with the coaching program itself. In some cases, schools have built programs they refer to as "coaching" programs but are really something else entirely.

Successful coaching is a humanistic, compassionate process that places the teacher and the students at its center, and good coaches foster supportive and productive relationships that improve student learning. Otherwise, we are just people who know some stuff and like showing off that we know it.

Even when a school has a solid coaching program in place, some teachers may still have reservations about working with a coach. To reach these teachers, coaches need to learn about the specific barriers they face and personalize their support in compassionate ways. To that end, each chapter of the book highlights one of the common barriers for teachers shown in Figure 0.1 and then offers strategies for implementing compassionate coaching in the corresponding focus area.

About This Book

Developing this book was an extensive process for us. We began by asking reflective questions: When did the people we coach most struggle? When was our coaching most successful, and to what could we attribute this success? Then we interviewed teachers, coaches, and school leaders we admire; developed working theses; and consulted peer-reviewed research to test our ideas. We revisited our favorite educational books, and we asked our personal learning networks what had made them excel at coaching. Our book is therefore built on the work of many people, and we are so appreciative to be part of such a thriving coaching community.

Although our focus is on *situational* barriers in this book, we are fully aware of the many existing *systemic* barriers to great teaching and learning, including issues related to school safety, discrimination, and inequity of resources. The help we offer here is intended to support, empower, and retain the human capital (the *people*) in our schools, but we acknowledge that systems also have an influence on both students' learning and teachers' work lives. We encourage you to get involved in organizations and movements that work to improve our educational systems. Advocacy is also an act of compassion.

Teachers are the most critical assets for ensuring that students learn effectively, and it is our pleasure to support them in compassionate ways to do their best work. Other coaches who walk this path will also find fulfillment in their work and, hopefully, come to see themselves as essential agents who make positive and lasting investments in their schools, communities, and society.

Thank you for taking this journey with us! We look forward to learning how this work plays out in your coaching practice.

1

Charting a Course for Effective Coaching

Most of the time, when we embark on a journey, our every action revolves around the destination. We enter the destination into our GPS to guide us, and we travel on the combination of paths we know will get us there successfully. The same is true of successful coaching journeys. The destination—effective coaching—comes first and foremost.

Of course, not all trips are smooth sailing. We hit distractions, roadblocks, and detours, and when we do, we need to focus clearly on the problem to see us through. The challenges keep us on our toes, but when we stay focused on the destination rather than the barriers, we are able to move forward. In this chapter, we'll discuss the essential elements of a successful coaching journey, including what you'll need to get going and some ways to help make sure your trip is a smooth one.

Setting Your GPS

Using a GPS is simple—you enter your destination, and away you go. If you get off track, your trip is recalculated to get you back on course using incremental steps. In coaching, you also need a system that can show you the way to your destination and get you back on track when you veer off course. This is where the Instructional Coaching GPS comes in; it's a reflective exercise for knowing exactly where you're going and how to get there. Whereas the GPS in a literal journey stands for "global positioning system," in the Instructional Coaching

GPS, the *G* stands for "goal," the *P* stands for "plan," and the *S* stands for "steps."

Goal
- What does instructional coaching mean to you?
- What are your hopes and dreams as an instructional coach?

Plan
- What daily actions will you take to adhere to your goal?

Steps
- How will you monitor or check that you are on your desired path?
- How will you course-correct if you are veering off your desired route?

Once you've written down your responses to the GPS questions, reflect on them. We have found that coaches need to be crystal clear on their work intentions if they are to stay the course on their journey, and your answers to the questions in the Instructional Coaching GPS can serve that goal.

Instructional Coaching Pathways

Just like journeys by road, effective coaching journeys require us to take certain tried-and-true pathways to reach our destination. In our vision of coaching, the three major pathways on the journey to success address the fundamental human needs of autonomy, belonging, and competence (Anderman & Leake, 2005).

The Autonomy Pathway

After decades of educational reforms, one of the major complaints teachers have is that their autonomy as practitioners is being steadily encroached upon. For example, in some schools, teachers are provided with a mandated curriculum. Although such a curriculum can offer a great instructional program for many students, some teachers say they have been discouraged from refining and adapting the curriculum to meet their students' specific needs. Teachers whose students must meet strict federal or state standards feel discouraged from using creativity or personalized goals with them. Too often, this lack of autonomy means coaches focus more on "fidelity" to the curriculum than on improving teacher practice.

Truly effective coaching places people above programs. Successful coaching isn't about bringing teachers along but about building teachers' capacity to make the right instructional decisions for students. Though coaches play an important role in probing teachers' beliefs about instruction and sharing research and strategies with them, individual teachers must have the freedom to tailor ideas for their classroom contexts and veto ideas they don't think they should prioritize. Put simply, teachers' autonomy is essential to the coaching journey.

Researchers Edward Deci and Richard Ryan (2000) have found that a sense of autonomy correlates with a sense of motivation. As Jim Knight (2019) writes, "People are rarely motivated by others' goals, and a one-size-fits-all model of change rarely provides helpful solutions for the individual complexities of each unique classroom" (p. 16). To Knight, being accountable to the detached vision of others is a kind of "irresponsible accountability," in contrast to the "responsible accountability" of teachers and coaches co-constructing goals and learning together through planning, discussion, and classroom-based coaching cycles (Knight, 2019).

The Belonging Pathway

Teachers who participate in coaching need to feel a real sense of belonging in the learning community if they are to succeed in their journey. This feeling is built over time, and each coaching interaction has the potential to build upon or erode it. One especially meaningful way to build trust is to honor commitments. If coaches don't show up or if they cancel their sessions, they can't expect teachers to respect what they have to offer. If a supervisor suggests that a coach cancel a coaching session to do something else, a frank conversation about the harm this could do to the coaching program is warranted.

The words and phrases we use as coaches can also have an effect on teachers' sense of belonging. It is paramount for us to come across as partners and learners rather than "experts," and one way to do this is to use proactive language (e.g., stems such as "I can," "I choose," or "I will"), both during coaching and in our own thinking about the process. (Figure 1.1 shows some easy ways to recast common phrases related to coaching with a more proactive slant.)

FIGURE 1.1
Proactive Coaching Phrases

Instead of...	Say or Think...
Teachers are not ready.	Teachers are not ready yet.
Teachers are reluctant to be coached.	Teachers fear the unexpected.
Teachers aren't willing to make changes.	Teachers need multiple opportunities to try out new strategies without being judged.
Teachers don't want to accept coaching.	Teachers will accept coaching when the process is clear.
I don't know how to reach teachers.	I can empower and support teachers.

Another way to ensure that teachers feel comfortable in the coaching process is to use what Garmston and Wellman (2016) call the "third point" (p. 109). This can be any focus of discussion separate from either the coach or the teacher: student work, a video of classroom instruction, a professional reading, a data set, and so on. A third point enables the coach and teacher to discuss and discover information and ideas together rather than the coach dictating what the teacher *should* learn or do (Knight, 2019; McKee & Davis, 2015).

The Competence Pathway

The most effective coaches revere the teaching profession and truly respect the competence of teachers. As Buckingham and Goodall (2019) note, "Learning rests on our grasp of what we're doing well, not on what we're doing poorly, and certainly not on someone else's sense of what we're doing poorly" (p. 7).

Lately, we've been intrigued by the concept of appreciative inquiry (AI) and the role it can play in framing strengths-based instructional coaching. "At its heart," write Stavros, Godwin, and Cooperrider (2015), "AI is about the search for the best in people, their organizations, and the strengths-filled, opportunity-rich world around them. AI is not so much a shift in the methods and models of organizational change; it is a fundamental shift in the overall perspective taken throughout the entire change process to 'see' the wholeness of the human system and to 'inquire' into that system's strengths, possibilities, and successes" (p. 97).

Appreciative inquiry moves us away from a deficit model of teaching focused on what isn't working toward a strengths-based approach that acknowledges the fundamental competence of teachers. At the center of AI is the 5-D Cycle, a reflective exercise composed of the following five questions:

1. **Defining:** What is a worthwhile focus for our collaboration?
2. **Discover:** What excites you about teaching / your content / your students?
3. **Dream:** How would you describe success?
4. **Design:** How do we design for success?
5. **Destiny (after a collaboration):** What were the successes we can repeat? How might we tweak this process in the future?

Think about how working through a path of AI shifts the focus away from deficits and toward shared success for students, teachers, and coaches alike. Whereas a deficit model rarely leads to the sense of competence needed for teachers to bravely tread new paths in their work, visions of success can serve to energize the work of change.

The Fuel

You can have your GPS ready to go and know the pathways backward and forward, but you aren't leaving the driveway unless there's gas in the tank. And just as cars need fuel to move forward, so too does instructional coaching. In our vision of coaching, this "fuel" is made up of three essential elements: the coach-administrator partnership, the coach's professional learning, and the coach's own willingness to be coached.

The Coach-Administrator Partnership

Administrator support of the coaching process improves the perceived value of the coaching process and, by extension, the number of teachers who seek coaching. For these reasons, we encourage principals to work closely with coaches in schools. Jim Knight (2018) offers the following suggestions for school administrators:

- Be sure the coach has time to coach and isn't focused on too many other duties.
- Encourage a partnership approach between teachers and coaches. Remember that the coach isn't there to "fix" anybody.
- Understand that, in most cases, coaches will maintain confidentiality about their work with teachers.
- Establish a schedule of regular meetings with the coach.
- Model an interest in professional learning for themselves.
- Remember that coaches are not supervisors (and that if they do have supervisory duties, those need to be made clear).
- Learn or develop a schoolwide set of instructional strategies.

Both parties should take time to sit down together and clarify each other's roles and responsibilities, and these touchpoints can form the foundation of any coach-administrator agreements.

One of the best ways for administrators to grow a culture of coaching in a school is by putting on their own coaching hats (Johnson, Leibowitz, & Perret, 2017), seeking out opportunities to reflect with teachers and share possible resources to help them reach their goals. A simple statement can go a long way. For example, say, "I understand you have a goal to help your students in the area of writing. Is there a certain book or resource you may need?" Suggesting that the teacher consult with a coach goes even further. At the same time, coaches should bear in mind that administrators often only have a big-picture understanding of the coaching process and may need to be told explicitly how to support the work.

Professional Learning

An abundance of books, training opportunities, and conferences addressing instructional coaching exist. Despite all these opportunities, we continue to encounter instructional coaches who had no formal training when they started coaching. We encourage you to fill your tank with as much knowledge as you can. Find a note-taking system that allows for mini-action planning as you learn.

One idea is the What, So What, Now What framework, which you can use to jot down key points, their importance, and your thoughts on how you can implement them. As you take notes, reflect on and answer these three questions:

1. **What** are the key points?
2. **So what** is so important about them?
3. **Now what** steps do I take to put them into practice?

We hope that reading this book will provide you with plenty of professional learning, but our words will never leave the page unless you put them into action. Let us know about your progress on Twitter, where you can find us at @KathyPerret and @kennycmckee, using the hashtag #compassionatecoaching.

Finding Your Own Coach

In a 2017 TED Talk, Atul Gawande reminds us that in sports, coaching is never over—everyone, even the top players, gets a coach. Therefore, if you're a coach, who coaches you? Finding a coach of your own can help you become a better coach yourself. Learning the importance of helping others reflect and grow is one thing, but experiencing the benefits firsthand is quite another. You deserve a confidant who will reflect with you just as you do with teachers.

Often, coaches will want to network with other coaches. We too think this is critical, but we also think it's vital to have a dedicated coach of your own. Michelle TeGrootenhuis, an Iowa-based coach, agrees:

> I began utilizing a coaching log when I realized I had no idea how much of my time was spent actually IN classrooms, working with teachers, versus gathering, analyzing, and sharing data and resources. However, tracking time was not by itself satisfying. I knew I needed to reflect on that information and then set some professional goals, but doing that on my own would not have been effective. I knew I needed someone else to look at that data and ask me questions, provide some feedback, and perhaps offer some suggestions. And, quite honestly, I needed someone to be an accountability partner, holding me to those monthly goals. I realized that as a coach, I needed a coach.

After working with her own coach, Michelle realized that coaching is more than resource accumulation, collaboration, and networking. Authentic coaching causes us to deeply reflect on our practice in order to become better coaches ourselves.

The Itinerary

As with any journey, instructional coaching works best with a well-planned itinerary in place. In the case of coaching, we have found that itinerary in the form of a three-phase cycle that includes (1) meaningful goal-setting, (2) core coaching actions, and (3) reflection. The coaching actions at the core of each cycle include co-planning, co-teaching, modeling, and observation (see Figure 1.2). Of course, not everyone needs to use the same itinerary to reach the same destination, and coaching cycles will look different depending on the situation. Elementary coaching cycles may look different than secondary ones, for example, and coaches serving a large number of teachers will have different cycles than those working with smaller faculties. For this reason, the three phases in Figure 1.2 are general and flexible enough to be adjusted, adapted, and applied as required.

FIGURE 1.2
The Instructional Coaching Cycle

Meaningful Goal-Setting
The teacher sets a goal that is meaningful to him or her and the needs of his or her students.

Coaching Cycle Core
Choose the appropriate coaching action based on the teacher's goal. Reflect and repeat.
Cycle through multiple coaching actions needed in order to reach the goal.

Co-Planning	Co-Teaching	Modeling	Observation
Teacher and Coach develop lesson(s) or units of study together.	*Teacher and Coach co-teach lessons, as needed, with the goal to expand the teacher's repertoire.*	*Coach models specific strategies teacher may need to see in action, and the teacher watches how students respond.*	*Teacher and coach construct observation protocol. Coach observes the teacher teaching and collects the agreed-upon information/data.*

Reflection
Teacher and Coach reflect on the process(es) used above. Reflection guides their next steps in the cycle.

One way to adapt the coaching cycle is to include only one or two coaching actions between the initial goal-setting stage and the final reflection stage. For example, in remote learning, coaches might engage only in the co-planning stage but examine student work with the teacher during the reflection stage. Content matters, too; a high school literacy coach modeling in a calculus or dance class may not be very helpful, for instance, so observation would make more sense.

Meaningful Goal-Setting

Coaching cycles typically begin with the teacher and coach determining a meaningful shared goal for the partnership—usually a student learning goal or an instructional practice goal. When helping to set a goal, coaches should be careful to avoid a deficit-model mindset. Rather than leading teachers down the path of what they or their students *can't* do, focus on strengthening what they *can* do.

An especially effective approach is for teachers to express their goal as a promise to themselves rather than as simply some outside metric they are trying to meet. For example, instead of setting a goal that all students will meet a certain state standard, a teacher might promise to incorporate a certain proven approach on a regular basis. These promises don't have to be on a grand scale; they simply need to matter to the teacher.

Meaningful Goal-Setting in Action

Mary came to the first meeting with her coach feeling very frustrated. She felt her class periods started out well, but they eventually declined to a chaotic mess by the end of the 50 minutes. Her coach invited her to describe the differences between the opening and closing of her class period. It was through this reflection that Mary realized that she had strong opening routines but was weak on closure. This was enough for her to set a promise for the coaching cycle: The coach and teacher would work together to set up a classroom routine for the end of class. Although the coach initially felt this promise was relatively trivial, once a strong closure was achieved, the teacher was ready to make other promises that had an even stronger impact on students. The initial promise taught her the power of coaching, making her ready for more.

Co-Planning and Co-Teaching

Once you've made a promise to yourself, some form of accountability can help keep you on the right track. Co-planning and co-teaching with a coach are particularly good ways to remain accountable during the coaching process.

In addition to supplying a form of accountability, co-planning can help equalize the coaching cycle, as it means both the teacher and coach are partners in the work. Co-planning with a coach can give teachers clarity on how to keep the promises they made in the goal-setting stage. As Saphier and West (2009) write, "Many teaching problems begin when teachers don't anticipate student confusions, can't figure out how to scaffold needed prior knowledge, and don't carefully think out experiences that would allow students to access new knowledge. In other words, many teaching problems begin with inadequate and unskilled planning" (p. 48). Indeed, to West and Saphier, planning should have "priority over observation and feedback conferences. Especially during the early days of building a coaching relationship, planning conferences offer more potential for improving instruction" (p. 48).

In co-teaching, the teacher and coach collaboratively plan the lesson and decide which role each will take in delivering the lesson to students. The coach may be more or less involved depending on the goals and needs of the classroom teacher. Afterward, the teacher and coach debrief the lesson and reflect together on strengths and weaknesses.

Co-Planning and Co-Teaching in Action

John recently made a promise to incorporate more ways to gain student engagement in his math classes, but he wasn't sure how to go about it. Together, John and his coach began to explore possibilities as a team, co-planning lessons and dividing up the classroom teaching and monitoring responsibilities. They also decided to video record lessons so they could capture what they couldn't always see in the moment. They were then able to reflect on each lesson with a sense of joint ownership, with each of them deeply invested in success.

The partnership gave John what he needed to stay accountable for the promise he made to himself. As for the coach, since this stage of the coaching cycle was taking a great deal of time, she allowed herself to engage in less-involved cycles with a few of the other teachers she was coaching. As the coach grew in her own capacity, she was able to maximize the co-teaching partnership by having other teachers visit and observe some of her co-teaching lessons with John. (In these instances, the group used an established protocol to reflect on the lessons afterward.)

Modeling

Sometimes a coach will teach students and have the teacher observe as a way of explicitly modeling certain strategies. Because the coach still recognizes the teacher as the expert when it comes to content and students, he or she shares lesson ideas and asks for suggestions during a pre-visit meeting. Although there is some co-planning, most of the planning is completed by the coach. During the class, while the coach is teaching, the teacher should collect data for further analysis and discussion. Afterward, the coach leads a reflective conversation with the teacher about his or her observations.

A word of warning when modeling lessons that we both learned the hard way: make sure teachers understand *why* you are coming in to teach a lesson and what their role is in the process. Unfortunately, we've had teachers actually leave the room or sit back and correct papers while we were attempting to model for them. To prevent this, we now co-construct look-fors and note-taking tools with teachers for us to examine jointly after the lesson is done. Setting up a reflective debriefing meeting ahead of time can also help teachers understand that modeling is not a break for them but, rather, a professional learning experience.

Modeling in Action

Fourth-grade teacher Gabriela was just starting a coaching cycle and knew she wanted to focus on collaborative structures with her ESL students to increase their language skills. In order for her coach to get a better understanding of the help she needed, they set up a time for the coach to observe her teaching a science lesson and collect some data about opportunity-to-respond rates. At the end of the lesson, Gabriela had her students respond to a writing prompt to determine their current understanding of the topic.

Next, Gabriela and her coach sat down with the opportunity-to-respond data and the responses to Gabriela's writing prompt. It was obvious to the teacher that the students who'd had more opportunities to respond had a better grasp of the content. Gabriela was drawing a blank on possible solutions and asked her coach for some suggestions. They landed on the Numbered Heads Together cooperative learning strategy, but

Gabriela wasn't comfortable using it without seeing it in action first.

The coach jumped at the chance to model the strategy for Gabriela. Following the coach's modeled lesson, the two of them planned and taught the next few lessons together. Soon Gabriela was ready to use the strategy on her own.

Observation

The purpose of classroom observations is to enhance the coaching cycle process. The coach and teacher establish goals for each visit, and during the observation the coach collects data as descriptively as possible. Often, a single observation is all that's needed to gather some baseline data for meeting the teacher's goal, with subsequent observations adding detail and nuance. Examples of issues that can benefit from classroom observation during the coaching cycle include lesson pacing, differentiation and equity, student engagement, questioning, opportunities to respond, student collaboration, and classroom routines.

Once the coach has collected observation data, the teacher should reflect on that information. This reflection process provides the teacher with a quick formative assessment of current practices and also helps to determine the next steps in the coaching cycle. Because observation does not require too much planning or additional work, it can be a good entry point for teachers with whom a coach has already built a positive relationship.

If coaches need to conduct their observations virtually, teachers can video record a relevant portion of their lesson and then upload it to a secure platform like Sibme.com. Some coaches record their coaching conversations with teachers as well. These kinds of objective records can help both the teacher and the coach assess student learning and the coaching process as accurately as possible.

It is important that teachers know exactly when the coach will be joining the classroom to observe them teaching, as unannounced observations can send the wrong message. They can feel evaluative, especially if teachers are only used to administrators watching them teach. If a coach needs to conduct observations outside of a coaching cycle to gather large-scale or generalized instructional data, any affected teachers must be told the time and purpose of the visits. Data collected in these cases should not be attributed to individual teachers but rather reported as whole school data.

Observation in Action

Antonne, a high school physical education teacher, wanted to improve his teaching approach. He felt his classes all followed the same format: minilectures followed by some type of physical activity. He knew there was more to teaching PE, but he just couldn't put his finger on the solution, so he reached out to an instructional coach for help. Though the coach was a little concerned that she did not have any experience teaching PE, she agreed to offer assistance.

The coaching cycle started with setting a goal to get a clearer picture of how students engaged with his lessons. To do this, Antonne and the coach decided that during an observation the coach would keep track of how many times students responded to questions during the minilecture. Due to the nature of Antonne's classroom—either a gym or large outdoor field—it was hard for him to see every student at all times, so the coach would circulate and take notes on what she observed. These notes coupled with Antonne's reflections led to a new set of goals, including creating stations for exercise-based activities and incorporating more frequent summarizing strategies for students during lectures.

Reflection

"The more reflective we are," Pete Hall and Alisa Simeral (2017) remind us, "the more effective we are" (p. 21). We believe there are four essential KEYS to ensuring that the reflection stage of the coaching cycle is empowering and inspiring for teachers (Perret, 2018b):

- **Keep it simple.** Reflection protocols and established routines can help with this. One strategy is simply to ask a teacher how he or she feels about a recent lesson. When in doubt during the discussion, you can always ask another question.
- **Engage in reflection.** To prompt the teacher, the coach might share student work or observation data and invite him or her to consider the implications for their progress.
- **Yield to others.** This isn't the coach's time to speak extensively. The teacher should talk for at least 80 percent of the reflection conversation time. Avoid using the word *I* during reflection conservations, and let the teacher take the lead when it comes to language usage (e.g., the names of specific instructional strategies). By making these concessions, we invite teachers to trust that our intentions are only to help them grow.
- **Stay focused on students and solutions.** Every reflective conversation should be centered on what's best for students and how to solve instructional challenges.

Roadblocks

Roadblocks and detours can get in our way during coaching just as they can during any journey—and as in those cases, we can either grumble through them or open our eyes to the possibilities a new route can offer. The rest of this book focuses on how to recast the six common teaching roadblocks mentioned in the introduction—lack of confidence, failure, overload, disruption, isolation, and school culture challenges—as opportunities for compassionate coaching. Now let's get started!

2

Coaching Through Lack of Confidence

I don't have the skills to do my best work right now.

Anne has been teaching 5th grade for 28 years. She has seen a lot of educational initiatives, approaches, and resources come and go; she even remembers using a ditto machine to run off copies. She has taught literacy using whole language, basal readers, reader's and writer's workshop, guided reading, and so on. She is a lifelong learner and takes the changes in stride, but over time they've eroded her confidence.

Anne's heart still lies in making a difference for each of her students, but she feels the pressure to stay current. Lately, she has expressed to the instructional coach in her building that she has never felt as inadequate as a teacher as she does today. How can a person with a master's in education and a reading and ESL endorsement carry this much self-doubt? She finds herself working harder than she ever has before just to stay current. She wants the best for her students, but her lack of confidence in her abilities weighs on her and is affecting both her professional and personal life.

✳   ✳   ✳

Mark is a second-year teacher, and his last class of the day is made up of freshmen who have been struggling to stay focused. He recently attended a session at a conference that describes the CHAMPs method of classroom management, but his initial attempts at implementing the approach haven't made an impact. He feels ineffective, and he thinks he isn't cut out for teaching. He wishes he had someone to help him

17

figure out how to better implement CHAMPs, but he doesn't want any-one to know he is struggling. He feels that it's vital to appear as though "everything's fine" to his administrators and colleagues.

*   *   *

The field of education is continually changing, with competing ideas and approaches spreading faster than ever before. Educators are scrambling to stay current while making an impact on student learning. Ever-changing acronyms are tossed around like a bowl of alphabet soup: Out with NCLB, in with ESSA! MTSS or RtI? STEM or STEAM? PBL, CBE, SEL, ABCDEFG—the list is endless, and the constant change can cause even the best teachers to doubt their own skills. Newer teachers, especially, can struggle with this issue, but it can affect teachers at any level.

Do you see fellow educators in your school who exhibit a lack of confidence? Do you feel a lack of confidence yourself as you take on the role of an instructional coach? If so, you are not alone. Over our years in education, we (Kathy and Kenny) have felt a lack of confidence both in our time as classroom teachers and as instructional coaches. It has stopped us in our tracks and pushed us beyond our comfort zones.

Looking back, a common denominator in both our journeys has been the support of others in our lives: mentors, coaches, administrators, fellow colleagues, and even students. We gained confidence when someone saw more in us than what we saw in ourselves. These individuals nurtured our strengths and helped us change our perspectives. It is largely because of them that we know focusing on partnership is an effective way to help teachers become more confident. When working with teachers who lack confidence, we focus on this Compassionate Coaching Focus of Partnership.

Helping Teachers Build Self-Efficacy

John Hattie (2016) defines Collective Teacher Efficacy (CTE) as the "combined belief of teachers in their ability to positively affect students" and ranks it first on his list of factors in student achievement, with an effect size of $d = 1.25$. Although building CTE takes time, it needs to start with individual teacher self-efficacy.

Albert Bandura (1994) first introduced the concept of self-efficacy, or "people's beliefs about their capabilities to produce effects" (p. 1). He found that people with high levels of self-efficacy were able to set and maintain challenging goals, and that they were able to quickly bounce back rather than let setbacks distract them. By contrast, Bandura found that those with low self-efficacy had low aspirations, weak commitments to goals, and a tendency to dwell on adverse outcomes.

As coaches, when we perceive a lack of self-efficacy in teachers, we must first reframe our own thoughts. These teachers need us, and they need us to believe in them. We can be their partners and strength-seekers, guiding them to identify strengths they didn't even know they had. (This is certainly what others have done for us throughout our careers. You wouldn't be reading this book if it weren't for all the coaches and mentors we've had in our lives who saw something in us before we saw it in ourselves.)

As Stephen Covey (2016) reminds us, we must seek first to understand, and only then to be understood. Our job is to be teachers' partners—not experts. Many teachers who appear resistant to coaching at first may simply lack confidence in their abilities, so we must be careful that *we* don't express a lack of confidence in them. A little self-talk prior to partnering with a teacher can help in this regard ("I believe Mary can do great things for her students," "Mary is capable of excellent instruction"). It also helps to reflect on the following questions:

- What strengths do I recognize in the teacher that I may be able to help them recognize over time?

- In what areas does this teacher exhibit more self-efficacy? Can that self-efficacy be translated to areas where confidence is lower?
- What factors in the school environment might be linked to this teacher's lack of self-efficacy?
- How can I provide sustained support and help this teacher set achievable goals?

Developing a Growth Mindset

Psychologist Carol Dweck, author of *Mindset: The New Psychology of Success* (2007), has provided us with the concepts of fixed and growth mindsets. Whereas those with a fixed mindset believe their talents and abilities are fixed in place and unalterable, those with a growth mindset believe in the power of hard work and continuous learning to overcome obstacles. By using language that encourages a growth mindset during the coaching cycle, coaches can help teachers understand that, with a little work and the right frame of mind, they can gain the confidence they lack. (Figure 2.1 shows ways coaches can reframe common teacher complaints using language aligned with a growth rather than fixed mindset.)

We must always be wary of fixed opinions and thoughts about teaching and learning. Sometimes the notion of "best" practices can lead us to a fixed mindset, as the idea itself implies that there is no room for growth. But there is *always* room to improve!

Devising Achievable Goals

Many teachers have persuaded themselves that they can't achieve the goals they set when the reality is that their goals are just too vague. Consider, for example, the goal "Get better at teaching." Well, we probably all feel that way, but how we might "get better" differs considerably for each of us. A high school special education teacher might want to better assess her students, yet a first-grade teacher might want to learn what apps would be most helpful for his students. Specifying what "better" looks like is important for creating plans to go with goals.

If you Hear...	Avoid Reframing with Fixed Mindset	Reframe with a Growth Mindset
FIGURE 2.1 **Aligning Language to a Growth Mindset**		
I am unable to reach these students.	I see what you mean. It is unfortunate students today are unable to grasp what we are teaching.	What are your hopes and dreams for these students? Let's work together to make them a reality.
That lesson flopped. I'll never be able to plan good lessons.	It's too bad. Maybe there are just certain activities you can't do with these students.	Did the whole lesson really flop? Which parts seemed successful? How can we build on those?
I can't use learning targets. There are too many things to teach. I cannot write them all down.	I see how writing all those targets might be overwhelming. Maybe we just don't worry about targets this semester.	I see that some of your goals are interrelated. What might be the primary outcome you want for students as a result of this lesson?

Another common issue with goals is that they are too ambitious. Take, for example, the goal "Digitize my entire curriculum." Meeting this goal would require hours upon hours spent creating new materials, scanning or digitizing past lessons, figuring out the learning management system, and so on. Limiting your goal to just one of these activities would be much more effective, allowing both teachers and coaches to see the impact of small shifts and changes.

One way for coaches to help teachers do this is by emphasizing the power of SMART goals—-that is, goals that are specific, measurable, attainable, relevant, and timely. Here, for example, is an excerpt from a recent coaching conversation Kenny had with a teacher:

Teacher: I cannot get my students to write anything longer than one- or two-word answers. I know the district wants to see students composing essays in social studies, but I'll never get them there!

Kenny: I see that you want them to do more writing. Going from one- and two-word answers to essays seems like a bit of a leap. What is the logical next step for your students?

Teacher: Well, writing complete sentences would be a good start!

Kenny: Yes, that sounds **attainable** from where they are. I think a response with a well-written sentence could be a **specific** goal for your students. Do you think that's **relevant** for their current performance?

Teacher: Yes, it would be. Do you think we could set that as a goal? "Writing complete sentences for responses to historical questions." I'm not sure how we accomplish that though.

Kenny: Have you used writing frames in the past? I think that we could begin by using writing frames for the next few lessons [**timely**], then see if more students are writing full sentences [**measurable**].

Teacher: I haven't used them, but let's see if we can try writing frames for their compelling question on the effectiveness of the Civil Rights Act of 1964.

Kenny: Perfect! Let's look at your lesson!

Notice how Kenny uses questioning and empathy to help the teacher develop a SMART goal. Although the teacher desperately wants her students to write essays, she feels like she is making progress by setting a micro goal for them to first write complete sentences.

Providing Sustained Support

When teachers are struggling, they need to continuously have access to a thought partner. How many of us have had the experience of learning something new and then falling short trying to implement it? Both of us remember many times in the classroom when we wished we had someone to turn to for support.

One recent study showed that sustained support is instrumental for improving the confidence of teachers, especially those who have transitioned to education from other fields (Pumo, Korreck, Hollis, Childers, & Zwadyk, 2019). Teachers reported a "significant increase in confidence in planning, instruction, and assessment with coaching support" (p. 41) when they received teacher-centered coaching, goal-setting, class visits for collecting data, and reflective discussion from their coach, and the retention rates of those for whom teaching was a second career leapt from 47 percent to 80 percent with the introduction of sustained coaching support.

Continuous support can feel overwhelming for coaches, but it really makes a difference. Here, for example, is a quote from a teacher who received such support from Kenny in his role as coach: "I have been fortunate to work with Kenny as my literacy coach since I started teaching and he has made an immeasurable impact on my instruction! He is reliable, collaborative, approachable, and intuitive of teacher needs." Notice how the teacher uses words like *reliable, collaborative, approachable,* and *intuitive.* These perspectives of Kenny as a coach are the result of sustained support.

By contrast, here's a teacher's response to a coach who did not offer sustained support: "I would not be opposed to or be annoyed by the coach periodically checking in with me, because sometimes I don't do a good job reaching out and tend to get too bogged down and don't know what kind of help I actually need." This teacher lacked confidence in the classroom in part because his coach wasn't consistently around to offer support. Being a partner means being there, which is why sustained support is so important for our teachers who feel a bit shaky.

Focusing on Questions

When working with teachers who lack confidence, it is important to gather as much information as we can about what is making them feel inadequate. Asking questions can help us—as coaches—understand teachers' knowledge, skills, and beliefs more intimately (McKee & Davis, 2015). For example, if a teacher says his students are not learning, rather than jump to conclusions as to why, the coach should ask for more information: "Tell me more. Can you give me some examples?" A simple opening question such as this places the coach as a partner working to solve a problem *with* the teacher.

Expressing Your Own Vulnerability

Although allowing ourselves to be vulnerable enables us to empathize with those we coach, some might find it counterintuitive, thinking it can make us look incompetent when we're supposed to be knowledgeable. In truth, our vulnerability can help teachers feel less alone and more confident. Modeling vulnerability and risk-taking are ultimately among the most effective things an instructional coach can do.

Vulnerable co-reflection is often the key to helping teachers who lack confidence take the first steps to investigate and enhance their practices. The strategy is simple. When talking with teachers about their own work, coaches should

- Ask for ideas to improve lessons or trainings.
- Share instructional mistakes they've made and how they addressed them.
- Communicate the challenges they see when focusing on how to support all students.
- Reflect on what they think helped and hindered learning after co-teaching or modeling.

Co-Planning and Co-Teaching at the Coaching Cycle Core

Be aware that the modeling stage can set the coach up as an expert; if the lesson goes well, the teacher may struggle to see how he or she could reach the same level. In addition, feedback from observations can be intimidating. By contrast, the co-planning and co-teaching stages require the instructional coach and teacher to work together as allies, boosting teacher confidence.

Co-planning and co-teaching can reveal the teacher's thought processes about instruction. The coach can then support the teacher's ideas with specific strategies or findings from the research. When teachers who lack confidence receive validation of their knowledge and skills from a trusted partner who wants to help fine-tune them, beautiful coaching successes emerge.

During co-teaching, both the teacher and the coach can formatively assess the effectiveness of their lesson together—either live in the classroom with the students or as a pair afterward, depending on the teacher's preference. For teachers who do not mind, reflection huddles with the coach while the lesson is in progress can be an exceptional growth experience.

Naming Teacher Strengths

To boost teacher confidence, coaches should take every opportunity to praise their strengths when they see them in action—what Jim Knight (2016) calls "being a witness to the good" (p. 115). For instance, imagine a teacher has received a poor evaluation and has been told to reach out to you for coaching. The teacher may feel he is not doing a good job for his students, and he may have mentally engaged in the cognitive distortion of overgeneralizing, viewing every component of his practice in a negative way. In such a case, you need to remember that the teacher might view you as a symbol of his weaknesses, so you should take every opportunity to emphasize his strengths instead. If you notice that he uses caring language with students in the classroom, for example, make a point to say so. Seeing that you have witnessed the good of his practice can shift his thinking about you; he now knows that you do not view him poorly.

Enhancing Your Own Confidence as a Coach

All coaches have moments of doubt in their practice. Here are a few strategies that you can use to help build your own confidence when necessary.

Lean into Research

Imagine the following scenario. You have been contacted by a colleague who is teaching a class with a lot of English language learners. She has used multiple strategies for supporting her students' English language acquisition. She has paired students with classmates who can help translate her directions for class activities, located translation tools that can help the students, and asked the school's ESL teacher to support students during their designated ESL class. Nevertheless, the students still seem unable to complete tasks, and they rarely approach her for help. She regrets that she does not know what to do next.

As the teacher describes her situation, you reflect on some of your own struggles to support English language learners and wonder if you could be of any service at all. What should you do?

The answer is to lean into research during the coaching cycle, studying the literature alongside the teacher you are coaching. For example, in this case, you may both learn the importance of sharing content and language objectives with English language learners so they have a way of framing their learning, or use World-class Instructional Design and Assessment (WIDA) performance standards to differentiate student assignments. Leaning into the research can strengthen the coaching process by providing a "third point" for influencing practice (see Chapter 1) and by offering the coach opportunities to engage in vulnerable co-reflection.

Use Coaching as an Opportunity to Grow

When both of us began our roles as instructional coaches, we first had to overcome a case of imposter syndrome—that sense that you're not really qualified to do what you're doing. It can feel like you have "tricked" others into believing you are capable, valuable, and worthy. This can lead some coaches to fake it—that is, to pretend they are experts on every topic that comes up (while secretly panicking on the inside). They work diligently to project expertise at every turn. No job is too big. No teachers' difficulties are *that* difficult.

Reacting in this way can be very harmful. Teachers will either see through the facade or be intimidated by such an apparently brilliant mind. When working with teachers who lack confidence, especially, coaches shouldn't *want* to act like they have it all together. If our role is to foster powerful learning, then we should model that learning ourselves, and coaching offers exceptional opportunities to do so.

We embrace Jim Knight's (2007) partnership principles of reflection and reciprocity, which suggest that educators need the time and space to evaluate how successful and sustainable their goals and practices are. Sharing that you are a reflective educator also helps you connect with others who are open to reflecting with you. When we view coaching as an opportunity for growth, we implicitly accept the principle of reciprocity—the belief that in coaching relationships, everyone learns and grows, including the coach.

We often find ourselves learning from the teachers we coach. In fact, we recognize that some of the teachers we work with are better overall instructors than we are! We could see their expertise as a threat if we chose to view it as proof of our inadequacies. Instead, we believe teachers' skill sets serve to complement our own. Effective coaching partnerships result in the positive growth of both individuals involved.

Be Open to Coaching

Like teachers, instructional coaches also need someone to help identify their strengths and partner with them on their journey. Simply put, we get better faster when we have coaches in our lives. Finding a confidant to reflect with is empowering and helps keep us accountable to our goals. It allows us to clear our headspace of negativity so we can focus on our work. Coaching for instructional coaches can take any of the following forms:

- **Local coaching.** Are there other instructional coaches in your area, either in your school or neighboring district? Setting aside time to reflect and set goals together can keep us on track and allow us to talk through our insecurities and create action steps with one another's input.

- **Global coaching.** Did you know you can connect with fellow instructional coaches every Wednesday evening at 9:00 p.m. EST? We would love to have you join the #educoach chat on Twitter—the longest-running chat on the platform for instructional coaches. Each week, we chat about a different topic of interest. Coaches from around the world have built their own professional learning networks by following and interacting on this chat. Reach out to us and we can help get you started. Our Twitter handles are @KathyPerret and @kennycmckee.

- **Self-coaching.** One powerful tool for self-coaching is the use of video. Recording ourselves in action has never been easier—it's as easy as tapping your phone. Think about an area in which you lack confidence as a coach. What could you record to collect a little data on yourself? Many coaches we talk to say they want a way to monitor their reflective questions and coaching conversations with teachers. Doing so (with the teacher's permission, of course) provides you with a concrete transcript of the conversation. You can then watch the video yourself to note both strengths and areas you might like to work on.

- **Virtual coaching.** Sometimes it helps to find a coach who is completely removed from your own setting and can point out issues others might not see. Virtual platforms such as Zoom, Google Meet, and FaceTime make this so easy. Kathy meets

virtually with coaches once or twice a month to help them identify and build on their strengths.

*　　*　　*

Although it's natural to feel unsure about ourselves as we work
through challenges, it can also have the danger of stopping us in
our tracks. By implementing the Compassionate Coaching Focus of
Partnership and the coaching strategies outlined in this chapter, you
can effectively support teachers to confidently approach challenges.
Coaches can help teachers boost their faith in themselves by serving
as a guide on the side, a partner, and a sounding board. It is our hope
that reframing lack of confidence as an opportunity for partnership
and implementing the strategies outlined in this chapter will allow
you to effectively support teachers in the coaching cycle.

3

Coaching Through Failure

I don't have the power to do my best work right now.

Diego has been in the field of education for 15 years. Throughout his tenure, he has received satisfactory to exceptional performance reviews. He has mentored new teachers as well as welcomed student teachers into his classroom.

This year feels different to him, though. He has been reading about ways to create student-centered classrooms, and he knows that having students take more ownership of their learning and having more opportunities to work together in teams will be beneficial for them. However, most of the new strategies he has tried have not worked well. At best, they feel clunky; at worst, students seem distracted and prolong every assignment much longer than he anticipated. He finds himself gradually retreating with each new problem that emerges. Where he once was reflective and ready to give new ideas a try, he now gives up easily.

Diego's coach has noticed he has become much more reserved over time, no longer sharing the new ideas he's trying. He expresses his frustration at how hard it has been to implement student-centered techniques in his classroom and worries that the poor results he is having with students might eventually affect his performance review. He even reveals to his coach that he has considered getting out of education altogether because of his lack of progress this year, although he still loves working with students.

*   *   *

Tina has more than 10 years' experience teaching U.S. history. She has a good rapport with students, uses innovative practices in her classroom, and is well known throughout her district for her leadership in disciplinary literacy for social studies and history. She was even nominated for Teacher of the Year last year.

This fall, Tina was called into the office by her principal who told her that her students' performance on the state assessment ranked below the growth expectations established by her state's public school accountability model. Though the principal is sympathetic, she is also concerned about the students' progress.

At first, Tina rejects the results but eventually acknowledges that her instructional decisions may have contributed to them. She had opted to teach some topics that don't address the standards for her subject, and she reflects that students seemed to struggle with more concepts this year than they had in the past.

She confides to her coach that she feels like a failure. She wonders whether all the success she had in the past was just a fluke. She no longer wants to share her ideas with colleagues in her district because she now feels like an imposter. She feels paralyzed about how she can move forward to improve her students' learning.

✹   ✹   ✹

Each of us has "evidence" that can "prove" our failures. For some, it's failure when the Wi-Fi goes out and they cannot teach their newest digital lesson; for others, it's when they've been placed on a formal action plan by an administrator. For still others, it's only failure when it's public—a poorly worded statement in a parent-teacher conference or students misbehaving when a colleague is in the classroom. We often hear people say they feel shaken by failure, which makes sense. Often, our foundations feel as if they have crumbled beneath us. In many cases, we have been blindsided by a person, place, or process we have always trusted.

Feelings of failure can emerge from internal or external sources. Internal sources include the comparisons we make between ourselves and others or the tension we may feel between expectations and experience. In the vignette at the start of this chapter, Diego feels like a failure because of the gap between his image of himself as an accomplished teacher and his struggles to reshape his classroom.

External sources that cause one to feel like a failure are a little different. An administrator may tell us we are not measuring up or our students may be underperforming on a standardized test. Tina feels this way when her principal meets with her about her students' test results. In these situations, we are often confronted with a difference between how we perceive our capacities and skills and outside evidence against that perception. Whereas internal sources of failure are subjective and intangible, external sources of failure take the form of harder "evidence."

Especially when coaching teachers who have encountered failure, we must focus on supporting their strengths. We want to erase the mindset that coaching is about fixing teachers. The Compassionate Coaching Focus of Empowerment frames our work around goals that will help the educators we coach reclaim their power in the professional growth process.

Being Mindful of Language

Language is an important part of dealing with failure, and the words we use can imply what our beliefs are, so one component of language is being mindful of how we speak. Our choice of words can even affect teachers' feelings about coaching. In a recent conversation with Phil Echols, senior administrator of professional learning in Wake County Schools in Raleigh, North Carolina, he used a phrase that we loved: "Our language can be spears or olive branches." What an eloquent way to describe the impact of language!

Most coaches *intend* for their words to feel like olive branches to teachers, but there are many ways we can unintentionally make them feel like spears instead. As mentioned in Chapter 2, we need to make sure we approach the teachers we coach with a growth mindset and use strengths-based language that communicates our beliefs about their competency and knowledge.

When teachers express feelings of failure, here are a few additional strategies for making sure your coaching language is as helpful as it can be.

- **Use the language of "yet."** Carol Dweck (2014) explains that when people encounter failure, they can either live in the "tyranny of now" or embrace the "power of yet." In much of Dweck's work, she talks about praising the process. Remind teachers that even though neither of you may have found the right path *yet*, you are committed to continuing to help them find it.

- **Ask to give feedback.** We should always ask teachers if they want to hear our feedback before providing it. Unfortunately, sometimes we are so eager to share our thinking that we interrupt teachers' thinking with our unwelcome contributions.

- **When you offer suggestions, give a few but not too many.** To empower teachers, we must respect and encourage their autonomy when it comes to instructional decisions. The best thing to do is share two or three ideas from research or from other teachers' successes and then ask the teacher which idea would work best for his or her students. If the teacher doesn't like any of them, explore new ideas together. Choice empowers teachers as experts.

- **Avoid all-or-nothing statements.** These statements are among the quickest ways to annoy and offend teachers. They are also usually inaccurate, fail to account for the diversity of processes and outcomes in schools, and undermine the knowledge and skills of teachers. Because they can be easily disproven by just a little research, all-or-nothing statements serve to erode trust and discourage productive discussions (McKee & Davis, 2015).

Encouraging Design Thinking

"Change is not a one-size-fits-all thing," writes Cornelius Minor (2019). "Nor is there a single solution or panacea for real progress. The work that is required feels like trial and error (and error and error) most of the time.... We are allowed to fail, reflect, improve, and try again. This is the only way" (p. 4). We believe the five-step design thinking process usefully incorporates this core truth, allowing us to successfully coach teachers through the inevitable failures of necessary trial and error in the classroom. Figure 3.1 provides an overview of the components of this process and how it can apply to instructional coaching.

FIGURE 3.1 The Design Thinking Process	
The Design Thinking Process	**What It Means for Coaching**
Empathize	Take the perspective of students (or colleagues, parents, whoever the solution is for).
Define	Define students' needs and your insights into the problem.
Ideate	Challenge your assumptions and create ideas for innovative solutions.
Prototype	Design lessons or strategies to solve the problem students are encountering.
Test	Test the lessons or strategies to determine their effectiveness and which aspects of the design process should be revisited.

Source: Inspired by information from "What Is Design Thinking and Why Is it So Popular?" by R.F. Dam and T.Y. Siang, 2020.

The design thinking process is iterative rather than linear. For example, once you test a solution, the results might provide more information about your students that would lead you back to the Empathize or Define phases; alternatively, while designing a lesson in the Prototype phase, you might return to the Ideate phase because you discover a new way to revise your approach that makes you reenvision how to move forward.

The process is an excellent protocol for helping teachers work through a perceived failure. Using it with teachers can support their empowerment as problem solvers again, and they might then teach their students to use the process for solving problems as well. Figure 3.2 shows sample questions coaches can use to support teachers while using the process during the coaching cycle.

A teacher who recently worked through the design process shared that she uses a quick two-question survey after she tries something new with her students. Coaches might also ask these two questions when they are modeling or co-teaching:

- What helped you learn today?
- What got in the way of your learning today?

Students tend to be forthcoming when asked these two questions, and this particular teacher did receive some critical feedback from students about wanting more interaction with one another during a lesson. After reflecting on this feedback, she returned to the Empathize phase of the design thinking process to note that students prefer more interaction. Then she worked through the design process again, making sure she planned for more frequent opportunities for students to interact throughout the next lesson she planned. Supporting greater interaction thus became a goal.

This teacher fully expects to receive critical feedback once more when she uses the two-question survey again in the Test phase of her next lesson, and again she plans to translate that feedback into a helpful goal. Now that she regularly uses the design process, she no longer sees student feedback as evidence of "failure" but as information guiding her next steps in the process.

FIGURE 3.2
Coaching Conversations Using the Design Thinking Process

Design Thinking Process Stage	Helpful Coaching Questions
Empathize	• How do your students feel about _____? • In what ways do they feel supported? • What engages or interests them?
Define	• What are your students' needs overall? • What challenges do they face in learning? • Which students need further interventions?
Ideate	• How would you teach if you were not afraid to fail? • How would some of your colleagues approach this situation? • If you could only make one change today, what would it be? • Are there any new insights that you have to this problem after the Empathize and Define brainstorming?
Prototype	• How could we design a lesson to teach this concept? • How could choice or differentiation support students' needs? • How could an assessment be used to determine how well the new approach helps students learn?
Test (after the prototype lesson/activity)	• What did students say about how they learned? • What did you observe about students during the lesson or activity? • What did the assessment reveal about their learning?

Focusing on Data as Information

Far too often, whether intentionally or not, administrators use student data as a tool to demean educators. Not only is this unkind, it's counterproductive because it makes teachers all the more resistant to learn from the data. We need good protocols in place for using data as information rather than evaluation.

"When we are analyzing data, we are placing students at the center of the discussion," notes Dr. Chaunté Garrett, superintendent at Rocky Mount Preparatory School in Rocky Mount, North Carolina. "We are looking for information about how they are progressing and what we can do to support them. When there is negative information, we shouldn't judge—let's just get to the bottom of it." We couldn't agree with her more.

Oftentimes, when teachers feel like they have failed, they struggle to accurately describe what is going on with their students. They may say they just aren't sure what's off, but they know *something* is. Or they might themselves use all-or-nothing statements such as "None of my kids are reading" or "All my kids are disengaged." By analyzing the data gathered during a coach's classroom observation, the teacher and coach can begin working together to determine strategies for improving student learning.

To organize classroom observation data, the teacher and coach might use any of these methods:

- Seating chart with text codes (such as *E* for engaged students, *Q* for students who asked questions, *N* for writing notes—whatever actions are being measured).
- Time markers (noting how much time each action or teacher activity took).
- Teacher-student talk table (a table divided into two-minute increments used to note whether teacher, students, or both are talking at any given point in the lesson).
- Scripting (used for teacher's questions or for recording student talk).

Early in Kathy's career, one of her goals as an instructional coach was to make sure teachers were comfortable when analyzing data. She was introduced to a brief from the Learning First Alliance entitled *Beyond Islands of Excellence: What Districts Can Do to Improve Instruction and Achievement in All Schools* (Togneri, 2003) that guided her work in this regard, especially the insight that districts make decisions based on data, not instinct. The brief outlines three actions districts have taken to ensure this:

1. They systematically gathered data on multiple issues, such as student and school performance, customer satisfaction, and demographic indicators.

2. They developed multi-measure accountability systems to gauge student and school progress.

3. They provided support to assist teachers and administrators in using data. (Togneri, 2003, p. 5)

The brief also suggests these three ways to facilitate data analysis:

1. Make the data safe.
2. Make the data usable.
3. Make use of the data. (Togneri, 2003, p. 5)

Kathy abides by these three tenets to this day when she works with both teachers and coaches. She also helps educators broaden their view of data, helping them see that it can take many forms: student performance data, baseline classroom data collected by a coach, student anecdotal records, formative and summative assessments, and much more.

To enforce the tenet of making data safe, Kathy uses the following four questions from Emily Calhoun (2001) during data analysis:

1. **What do you notice when you look at these data?** (This question is just about the facts, not opinions.)

2. **What additional questions do these data generate?** (Be careful that questions are about the data and not external factors.)

3. **What do these data indicate students need to work on? Based on these data, what can we infer teachers need to work on?** (See if participants can connect student evidence directly to instructional practices, classroom structures and schedules, or curriculum materials).

4. **What do the results and their implications mean for your school, district, or regional improvement plans?** (This

question implies ACTION. In using these questions with an individual, reframe to ask what do the results and their implications mean for you.)

Taken together, these four questions serve as an excellent protocol for objective, nonjudgmental data analysis. In fact, Kenny adapted them, along with the tenets from the First Alliance Brief, to create a data analysis protocol for his school district, Buncombe County Schools in Asheville, North Carolina (see Figure 3.3).

After using the protocol, the team analyzing the data applies what it learned to create a student achievement plan such as the one in Figure 3.4. Notice how each goal in this plan includes specific actions and the people responsible for them. This particular plan helped to greatly improve student achievement on the end-of-course test. Though the plan has worked well, the data-analysis team still revises it periodically based on new insights about each new batch of students.

Coaching in the Context of a Poor Teacher Evaluation

One of the most difficult circumstances for a coach and a teacher occurs when the coaching relationship becomes the center of a dreaded action plan that has resulted from a poor teacher evaluation. Sometimes, prolonged disappointment and concern over a teacher's performance forces an administrator's hand to make a plan for that teacher's improvement. The consequences of not showing improvement on the plan are often serious, including termination.

This situation is especially difficult in terms of coaching because it potentially places the coach in the position of an evaluator, at least in the eyes of the teacher. He or she might see the coach as someone who is "collecting evidence" for his or her own dismissal, which does little to build the trust necessary for the coaching process to work. A maxim applies here: "The coach's role is to help teachers see the light. The administrator's role is to make them feel the heat." Of course, administrators help teachers "see the light," too. However, in the case of an action plan, the administrator is unquestionably turning

FIGURE 3.3
Data Analysis Protocol

1. What is the data measuring?

2. What observations can you make? (Let's hold off on inferences for now.) Use the chart to note observations.

3. What inferences can you make? (What might be causing what we have observed?) Use the chart to note inferences.

Observations (Question 2)	Inferences (Question 3)

4. What do we have influence or control over?

5. Based on what we have analyzed, what actions could we take?

Goal	Actions	People Responsible

Source: Used with permission from Buncombe County Schools, Asheville, NC.

up the heat, and both parties must agree that the coach's role is to support the teacher's improvement—not to become what Kenny calls "the Pink-Slip Angel."

FIGURE 3.4
Earth Science Team Student Achievement Plan

Goal	Actions	Persons Responsible
All earth science students read and write every day.	• Plan daily reading and writing activities. • Utilize successful practices such as creating text sets and using Newsela. • Integrate guided reading of complex texts at least once a week.	Teacher Team and Coach
Smaller, more specified units.	• Chunk large units into sets of smaller, more focused units. • Clarify and share learning targets for each unit. • Identify and teach essential vocabulary for each unit.	Teacher Team
Continue integration of challenging activities.	• Use presentations, projects, and labs regularly because they have impacted the growth of all students. • Refine scaffolding practices to ensure that lower-performing students are challenged in appropriate and supportive ways.	Teacher Team and Coach
Investigate strategies for improving achievement of female-identified students in science courses.	• Look for high growth in female student subgroups in earth science classes at other schools in the district. • Compile research on increasing girls' achievement in STEM. • Share results of research with the earth science team on an ongoing basis.	Coach

Source: Used with permission from Buncombe County Schools, Asheville, NC.

Many teachers are first informed of being on an action plan when an administrator tells them the coach will be coming by to see them. Red Alert! We can tell you from our own experiences, coaching that starts this way is a dead end. These teachers will never trust a coach who shows up to "check up on them." Instead, we stress that administrators need to tell the teacher to reach out to the coach. When teachers contact coaches for support, regardless of the impetus, they will be much more receptive to coaching.

Facing Failure as an Instructional Coach

A sense of failure is unfortunately quite common for instructional coaches and teachers. We know the feeling firsthand. Do any of the following sound familiar?

- Teachers don't seek you out for coaching.
- A coaching cycle didn't go as you thought it would.
- You are expected to support the implementation of a new initiative that is being met with resistance.
- You've had what you felt was a successful coaching cycle, but the student data don't reflect it.
- Coaching cycles are supposed to be your main priority, yet you never seem to have the time to even make them happen.

Chances are you can add even more to this list. When we feel a sense of failure, the important thing is to focus on what is in our control. Luckily, there are two actions you can take that can help you to do this: engaging in positive self-talk and leaning on mentors.

Engage in Positive Self-Talk

Positive self-talk is incredibly important when we encounter failure. It is about more than our work; it is also about our overall health. The effects of positive self-talk include increased vitality, greater life satisfaction, and less stress and distress (Holland, 2020). Negative self-talk, especially among those who have experienced failure, is often a manifestation of cognitive distortions. Figure 3.5 shows some common cognitive distortions (Burns, 1989) associated with negative self-talk and ways to reframe that self-talk in a positive way.

FIGURE 3.5		
Sample Positive Reframings of Negative Self-Talk		
Cognitive Distortion	**Negative Self-Talk**	**Positive Self-Talk Reframe**
All-or-Nothing Thinking *Viewing a situation as a total failure if it is not perfect*	"Because I can't meet this one expectation, I have totally failed as a coach."	"Look at all I've accomplished. This is just a challenge for now."
Emotional Reasoning *Believing a negative feeling/thought is tied to a reality*	"I don't feel like going in today. I must be a horrible coach."	"Why am I feeling this way? Am I stressed, tired, or worried? What can I do to meet my needs?"
Jumping to Conclusions *Interpreting a detail as negative with no evidence*	"My colleague looked like he was frowning when I shared ideas in the meeting. He must think I'm an idiot."	"I have no idea why he was frowning."
Magnification *Exaggerating the size of a problem*	"Ms. Smith told me that my workshop was old information for her. It must have been a waste for everyone."	"Most of the teachers' feedback was positive. Perhaps I can find ways to personalize elements of workshops."
Labeling *Assigning a label to yourself or others based on a fleeting event*	"I am a failure."	"Everyone experiences struggles."

Knowing you are experiencing cognitive distortions is half the battle. Once you can identify them, use positive self-talk and reframing to bring your thoughts to a more compassionate—and realistic—place.

Lean on Mentors

Ironically, many coaches feel as if seeking their own coach makes them look like failures.

When we feel like we are failing, leaning on a mentor can mean the difference between sinking and staying afloat. We don't mean the official mentors that are sometimes assigned to new teachers, coaches, or administrators, although those relationships can be incredibly beneficial. We mean mentors that we personally select.

We see a mentor as a special type of coach. Whereas a coach usually helps people reach specific goals within a given time span, a mentor is someone with whom you have a long-term relationship and in whom you can confide on a personal level. A mentor makes a commitment to support a mentee's growth in every area. Although a mentor's experience is highly valuable to a mentee, he or she does not necessarily have to work in the same role or even organization (Gazzara, 2019).

When we asked Dr. Chaunté Garrett what she looks for in a mentor, she told us she seeks out "those with both wisdom and context" who have been through similar situations and who understand her circumstances. We also asked members of ASCD's Emerging Leader program about their experiences with choosing mentors and discovered several patterns. Although a few had formally asked to be mentored, most had not. They usually discovered their mentors through a working relationship. Sometimes, a former principal or supervisor became a mentor. Others worked with the teachers in teacher teams or PLCs or even on projects outside their own schools or districts, such as state committees or professional organizations. However, in all cases, the mentors and mentees had worked together before, so they had knowledge of what each valued and contributed. Here are some of the qualities these educators told us they looked for in a mentor. Good mentors are

- Open to vulnerability
- Honest

- Transparent
- Trustworthy
- Master educators
- Able to build self-efficacy
- Able to see mistakes as part of the process
- Committed to helping you find solutions

We must remember that a mentor-mentee relationship is two-sided. Alissa Farias, an assistant principal in Tacoma, Washington, says her mentors were "thinking partners and they knew I was open to feedback. This opened up doors for them to push me and challenge me. They would never tell me what to do but instead did a lot of wondering, so I would always discover my own answer."

*   *   *

At the beginning of this chapter, we noted that the experience of failure is difficult no matter what the "evidence" of failure is or how we personally define it. When we coach educators who have experienced failure in the classroom, we should use the Compassionate Coaching Focus of Empowerment so they can move forward in their work.

4

Coaching Through Overload

I don't have the time to do my best work right now.

Erin is a high school biology teacher working in a traditional public school. She has seven years of experience, and she has felt established in her confidence as a teacher over the last few years. She has worked with her fellow teachers to create a pacing guide and curriculum that makes sense to them as a team. Everything seems to work pretty well, although some students still struggle with some concepts in her class.

However, this year, the school's performance grade has dipped from years past. The district has suggested a focus on writing to learn for all secondary schools. In the meantime, the school's principal is focusing on a rubric for student engagement that the principal, coach, and fellow teachers will use during class visits to provide feedback on levels of engagement. In addition, the district science specialist has asked teachers to begin using a new online textbook.

Erin's head is spinning. She wants to do a good job, but she is at a loss as to how she can excel at everything on her plate. She is experiencing what is known as initiative overload. She knows all these new initiatives are important, but how can she keep up her daily workload (and personal obligations, for that matter) while also making progress on these goals that compete for her time and attention?

✳   ✳   ✳

James is a young teacher with three years under his belt. He has enjoyed working with his 7th grade students in his English language arts class, and he loves to look for new strategies and texts to engage them in learning. He is what's known as an early adopter—willing to try any task he believes will benefit his students. He pursues professional learning on his own in addition to taking full advantage of what his school provides. He often approaches his coach for support (which his coach appreciates greatly).

However, James is starting to experience some anxiety. He decided to pursue National Board Certification this year, which he admits is a much more time-consuming process than he first imagined. He also signed up for an online MOOC-Ed on disciplinary literacy that has weekly assignments to complete. He has become involved in Twitter chats on adolescent literature and English language arts. He enjoys learning in these communities, and he feels deeply regretful if he misses any of the chats.

James is experiencing self-overload. Although he shows many indicators of being an educator who is invested in professional growth and teacher leadership, he is quietly burning out, trying to keep up with all of these opportunities.

*   *   *

Time. To many educators, it is the single most valuable resource available to them. Unfortunately, it can also often feel like the rarest.

Some teachers live in a constant day-to-day race to get as much done as they can while outrunning all the "time thieves" that surround them. These thieves can take many forms: a long faculty meeting, a fundraiser, a pep rally, a chatty colleague—and, let's be honest, time spent with an instructional coach. We hate that some teachers view working with us as "just one more thing," but almost all of us have had that experience.

We believe that the Compassionate Coaching Focus of Prioritization can drastically mitigate the state of overload so many teachers feel today. The more strategic and focused teachers are, the less likely it is they will become lost in the whirlwind of their teaching lives. In this chapter, we'll explore central aspects of prioritization for over-loaded educators—determining the most important goals, allocating time effectively, encouraging self-care, and creating space for reflection—plus an assortment of additional strategies coaches can use to enhance their own work.

Determining the Most Important Goals

When everything you do (or want to do) as a teacher is a blur, how do you even start to determine your most important goals? One thing we can do as coaches is help teachers engage in the practice of priority listing.

The coach starts by asking the teacher to list all current goals, giving him or her a few minutes of quiet time to get everything out. Once the teacher is done, both the coach and the teacher examine the list together. Sometimes these lists are quite exhaustive; other times, the teacher may only be able to generate a few items. Numbering the goals brings some clarity to the process. If the list is shorter than anticipated, the teacher might feel more capable of meeting all the goals. Sometimes our thoughts have a way of multiplying the size of our worries!

The next step is for the coach to ask the teacher which goal on the list feels the most *pressing*—that is, which one needs to be met most immediately. The purpose of doing this is to identify the teachers' primary stressor. Sometimes the goal can be taken care of quickly, lifting the teacher's mental cloud. For example, the goal might be to finalize tomorrow's lesson. In such a case, this should become top priority for the coaching session, and the pair can return to the list later. If the teacher feels the goal is not so pressing that it needs to be met today, then it should be marked with a 1.

Next, the coach asks the teacher which goal feels most *important*. This is usually something more meaningful for the teacher's overall goals and is usually centered on the curriculum or classroom instruction. Sometimes what is most pressing is also most important, which is great because it sharpens the focus of the coaching session. If there is a different goal that emerges from the "most important" question, this goal should be marked with a 2.

In the third step, the coach asks the teacher to identify another goal that would make a difference to students. This question invites the teacher to select a goal that may not be urgent but that is centered on students. The answer to this question often reveals the teacher's passion for meeting students' needs. If the teacher can't think of a goal that's neither pressing nor urgent, that's alright—fewer goals mean greater focus. If there is a third goal, though, it might be worth examining in the future. Label this goal with a 3.

The final questions are meant to cross out goals. Here, the teacher examines the list and answers these questions for each goal:

- Are there serious repercussions for me professionally if I let go of this goal?
- Do I have the time right now to meet this goal?
- Will meeting this goal improve the quality of my day-to-day work with students?

If the answer is "no" for all three questions, then the goal should be crossed off the list for now. For some teachers, these last questions can drastically reduce their list. These "non-goals" are really distractors that can be relinquished so the teacher can focus on what matters most.

Any goals that are neither numbered nor crossed out can stay on the list; they just aren't the focus of the moment. We call these the "not nows." It may be worth pursuing these goals in the future, but in order to move forward on the most pressing and important matters, they need to be tabled for now.

The teacher can post this priority list where it can be referenced often, such as in a plan book, on the wall beside the teacher's desk, or in a convenient digital form. When the teacher is overwhelmed, he or she can return to the list to ground the work. Of course, after having met the top one to three goals, the teacher can return to the list and identify the next round of goals to focus on. The coach, meanwhile, should consider ways to help the teacher along the way.

Allocating Time Effectively

For teachers who are overloaded because they have trouble allocating their time properly, coaches might introduce the "rocks" demonstration—a relatively simple visualization exercise that was popularized in Steven Covey's *The 7 Habits of Highly Effective People* (2016). Here's how it works. You are given a large empty container and three smaller containers: one that holds large rocks, another with smaller pebbles, and the third with sand. First, you pour the sand into the empty container, followed by the pebbles. When you try to add the rocks, you find that they won't fit. However, if you reverse the order—if you put the rocks into the empty container first—it all becomes easier. The pebbles come next, filling in the spaces between the rocks, and the sand fills in the tiniest spaces. Suddenly, just by what came first, everything fits! Transferring this lesson to daily schedules, teachers can think of the big rocks as the goals marked 1 on their priority list, the pebbles as the goals marked 2 or 3, and the sand as the "not nows."

Encouraging Self-Care

Talking about self-care with teachers might seem a bit touchy-feely to some coaches, but this book *is* all about compassionate coaching, and we think it's worth trying if it'll help teachers deal with overload. Coaches are not counselors, but what we are advocating is that coaches check in with teachers, ask about how they are handling their workloads, and encourage them to incorporate self-care practices into their day.

Sometimes coaches can create opportunities for self-care during the session itself. For example, a walk-and-talk meeting can help teachers get some exercise and stretch while brainstorming and reflecting—around the school, perhaps, or outside if the sun is out. Both exercise and sunlight are good for our mental health, so why not get a little of both during the school day? Another option to "get away" for a bit is to have an after-school coaching session at a coffee shop. Sometimes a less formal setting can help unleash creative thinking about our goals, and having coffee together is a great way to bond over other shared interests and build a deeper relationship.

Making Time for Reflection

Reflection is well-established as an important way to process learning into long-term memory and to set specific goals for the future. It's even embedded in Proposition IV of the National Board for Professional Teaching Standards' Core Propositions: "Teachers think systematically about their practices and learn from experience" (n.d.). Unfortunately, overloaded teachers will often sacrifice this important part of the learning process to meet short-term goals.

If we are committed to everything, with every minute of our days allocated to others, when do we have time to actually internalize our experiences? We certainly don't. However, creating intentional space to reflect is essential if teachers are ever to go from simply checking tasks off a list to experiencing deep personal and professional growth. And since reflection can feel static to the ever-busy educator, coaches must try getting them to see that it is *already* on their to-do lists—they need to find the time for it at some point!

Micro-Modeling

We first read of the micro-modeling concept in Diane Sweeney and Leanna S. Harris's *Student-Centered Coaching: The Moves* (2017). Here's how they explain it:

> Micro modeling is a strategy where a coach models a small portion of the instructional block rather than the whole thing. It serves the important role of providing visual examples for teachers while also allowing the coach and teacher to share ownership over what is taught, something that is often missing when a coach is up in front of the room and teaching her heart out for an entire lesson. (p. 76)

For many teachers who are overwhelmed, relying on the coach to demonstrate a particular instructional practice can make learning much easier. They can see specifically how the practice is introduced to their own students, how their students react to it, how well students grasp the concepts and content, and how they might implement the practice on their own.

As Sweeney and Harris note, a lot of classroom modeling involves the coach teaching an entire class period. Even though having the coach "take over" a class can certainly make an overwhelmed teacher's day in the moment, it may not help the practice being modeled transfer to the teacher's own practice. Whoever is doing the work (as well as the thinking) is usually the person doing the learning. In addition, if a teacher feels stressed, the process of co-planning an entire lesson is not optimal.

Micro-modeling allows the coach and teacher to avoid these problems. Modeling a single, clearly defined practice also leads to a quicker, more focused debrief of the coaching cycle, which is often advantageous to the overloaded teacher. For example, in a recent coaching partnership, Kenny worked with a teacher who wanted to shift her vocabulary instruction to enable students to determine the meanings of unknown words in a text. The two of them discussed the power of morphological knowledge to unlock the meanings of complex words. Kenny suggested a research-based generative process of working with morphemes that the teacher found intriguing, but she had trouble visualizing how to use the process in minilessons with students. They decided that Kenny could model the process in the first 20 minutes of each of her classes on a specified day. Then they would use her planning time at the end of the day to reflect on the process and the impact it had on her students' understanding.

Following the "Innovate Like a Turtle" Approach

Teacher and instructional technology director Vicki Davis (2016) came up with the idea to "innovate like a turtle," which we think is perfect for using with teachers who self-overload. Innovating like a turtle means setting aside 15 minutes two or three times a week to learn a new skill focused on a single goal at a time. For teachers who put pressure on themselves to always be at the forefront of new strategies and tools, this practice can support innovation while also helping prevent burnout.

Using Time Creatively

One way we can tailor our coaching to the needs of overloaded teachers is by being creative about how we use our time. When Kathy served as a literacy coach in a K–5 building, she discovered a helpful way to do this. One day, as she watched two teachers sit in on a 30-minute "reading buddies" session where upper- and lower-grade-level classes partnered to read together, she wondered if both teachers really needed to be present in the room. Could she find a nearby place where she could engage one teacher in part of a coaching cycle such as co-planning, while the other teacher remained present in the classroom with the students? She mentioned this idea to the two teachers and got their input. Both were receptive, but they wanted to make sure students understood the process well enough before leaving one teacher alone with all the students. The three of them co-planned a few lessons to explicitly teach students, and this creative use of time resulted in Kathy finding opportunities to meet with each teacher twice a month.

Thinking outside the box when it comes to time is useful in all kinds of settings for alleviating overload. Perhaps there are times middle school or high school classes could partner with elementary students, for example, freeing up some teachers for coaching. Alternatively, if high school students are studying child development, maybe they can partner with younger students to engage them in some sort of learning experience.

Kenny has used a couple strategies to use time creatively with teachers. For example, at one point he was working with an English teacher to develop some new approaches to grammar instruction. Several other teachers were interested in experimenting with the method he and the classroom teacher were trying, and many of them asked if he would be willing to model the lesson in each of their classes after he co-taught it with their colleague. Realizing that this would take a lot of time on his part and knowing that he wanted the teachers to personalize the approach for their own students, Kenny and his co-teacher proposed an alternative. What if each of the teachers visited for part of their planning period to observe them teaching the lesson? This would give them a good understanding of the lesson's sequence and strategies as well as the freedom to decide whether they found it worth pursuing. As a bonus, they could give feedback to Kenny and his co-teacher! A single day of co-teaching also became a modeling *and* a group reflection cycle, condensing and saving time for everyone involved. Of course, for this to work, all parties need to be comfortable in combining the cycles, but many teachers like the unique opportunities combinations such as these can present.

Another idea is to combine two classes if they are small enough. Once, a teacher asked Kenny to model a Paideia seminar for her students and suggested that a colleague down the hall might also want to join. Combined, their classes would be about 30 students—could he do the seminar with all of them? Of course! Sure, Kenny had some concerns, but he also realized that any potential issues arising during the seminar would be a wonderful grist for the post-modeling reflection!

Some schools schedule time for professional learning communities (PLCs) to meet. If a group of teachers expresses interest in coaching, coaches can offer to work with them during their regular meeting time. Kenny finds that setting up monthly or biweekly meetings is helpful, because this way, teachers feel empowered to lead the PLCs when he is not there—but he can still provide guidance and support when they seek it.

Establishing Your Priorities as a Coach

Just as teachers need to prioritize their goals, so too do instructional coaches. Establishing a coaching priority will allow you to monitor where you exert energy. One of the best parts of coaching educators is that we have the opportunity to personalize our support based on their identified needs. Conversely, one of the most difficult parts is that sometimes we can see needs that they have not yet uncovered themselves. Casually weaving your coaching priority into coaching conversations, planning, co-teaching, modeling, or resources allows you as the coach to move forward on your priority in a consistent and inviting way that does not announce to teachers that what they are doing is "wrong."

Matching Your Actions to Your Priorities

Joellen Killion and Cindy Harrison (2006) have outlined 10 distinct roles that teacher leaders and coaches play in offering support:

1. Resource Provider
2. Instructional Specialist
3. Curriculum Specialist
4. Classroom Supporter
5. Learning Facilitator
6. Mentor
7. School Leader
8. Data Coach
9. Catalyst for Change
10. Learner

We can often find ourselves dipping into each of these roles, and many of us feel we must be able to do all of them both simultaneously and well. However, Killion (2019) emphasizes that we should take on roles that align with the goals of our coaching and that these goals will shift over time as our priorities do.

In one of Kenny's schools, the coaching priority was to help teachers increase the volume of writing in all classrooms in the school. To make progress on this goal, he needed to align his actions to it. This resulted in him focusing his work around four of the roles for the school year. First, his priority dictated that he must take on the role of (1) learner first—he needed to be aware of how writing may differ from subject to subject, what the research said about the impact of writing on learning, and a few high-yield writing routines and strategies that could be used across a school. Once he had learned, he had to provide professional learning opportunities to faculty, playing the role of (2) learning facilitator. He had to be able to help teachers use new writing practices by providing them with ideas, templates, and rubrics—making him a (3) resource provider. Finally, he needed to use coaching cycles that focused on writing whether he was modeling, co-teaching, or providing feedback during class visits. These last areas called on him to be a (4) classroom supporter.

Expressing Gratitude

Regularly practicing gratitude can improve the speed with which we develop trusting relationships, the quality of our psychological health, and our ability to be resilient (Morin, 2015). It is a major component of healthy self-care for both teachers and coaches. Although we all may very well need to have less-demanding workloads (and life schedules overall, for that matter), reframing how we view our busy schedules can change how we feel about them.

For example, if you find that you are overloaded with coaching requests and feel stressed about a lack of white space in your schedule, consider maintaining a gratitude journal and keeping track of what you're grateful for. You might write, "I am grateful that so many people value my expertise and want to work with me," for example, or "I am grateful that my workload ebbs and flows, and that I will have less work or a break soon," or "I am so thankful that my colleagues trust me to ask me to support their work."

If you have a fairly long-standing relationship with a teacher you coach, we recommend sharing some of your perspectives on gratitude and how it shifts your thinking and lowers your anxiety with them. Many teachers with whom we have worked have found value in this practice. We know that to some people this may sound hokey, but we have learned from personal experience how much expressing gratitude can help when we feel overloaded.

Organizing Your Calendar for Success

First of all, if you are a coach without a calendar, you need to get one today! Seriously, stop reading right now and pick one up. It can be a print or digital calendar, but you need to have one. Here's why: your calendar is essentially a road map of your intentions and commitments. If you are trying to coach without a calendar, you may not be clear on your priorities and the actions necessary to meet them. With no clear sense of priorities, you have no idea whether you are being successful or not. You also run the risk of trying to remember your commitments to others.

In our experiences, there are three key calendar practices that can support your sanity as a coach:

1. Write down every priority and commitment you've made.
2. Schedule preparation time into each day.
3. Hold white space for reflection time at least once a week.

Eager coaches often suffer from the problem of overscheduling their calendars. Let's face it, when you are a new coach, you are often dreaming and begging for coaching collaborations. These early "starvation" days of coaching can make you feel like you must spend every second of the day serving others until your coaching picks up. However, good coaching requires preparation. You need time to create lessons, research resources, prepare for post-observation discussions, plan professional learning experiences, gather data for PLC supports, and many other duties. Expect to create a space in your day to do these things—but not *all* day. One of the benefits of blocking out planning time is that such time is flexible—you can move it around your schedule as best suits your priorities.

Practicing Weekly Reflection

Both of us understand the resistance many teachers feel when we suggest reflecting at least once a week. With so much to do and so little time, why would anyone waste an hour or more each week on something as amorphous as reflection? The answer is that reflection is essential, both for us to grow and for us to appreciate our accomplishments. One method for reflecting is to simply make notes of patterns you see over the course of a week of coaching. You may notice shifts in the requests you receive from teachers. You might be making an impact with a certain new strategy or protocol. You might notice that teachers are responding well to co-teaching, showing faith in that stage of the coaching cycle.

Another method of reflection might be to review your calendar again and write a brief reflection about the highlights of the week and your next steps. Reviewing the highlights can help you see the impact of your work on a regular basis. So many coaches talk about working all week, arriving home exhausted on Friday, and asking themselves, "Did I do anything that mattered this week?" Of course, what we do every week matters; we just forget about how impactful it is if we don't make time to review it.

It's helpful to turn reflections into goals. Sometimes these can be logistical, as in "Be prepared for the leadership team on Monday." Other times, they could be based on bigger ideas. For example, say you learned about a new protocol for conducting a coaching cycle at a recent workshop. You could make the next step to try the new protocol for the next three coaching cycles in order to see if it works better than your current protocol. Without creating white space on your calendar for reflecting each week, you may lose these opportunities to celebrate your successes and take charge of your future actions.

✳   ✳   ✳

Feeling overloaded is far too common a barrier—and it's one that prevents teachers and other educators from doing their best work. It can also lead to the much more dangerous state we call burnout. Coaches can help teachers prioritize their goals, time, self-care, and learning so they can surface from the abyss of overload. By implementing the Compassionate Coaching Focus of Prioritization and the coaching strategies outlined in this chapter, you can effectively support teachers to become more focused and less stressed, resulting in better teaching and learning for their students.

5

Coaching Through Disruption

I don't have the processes to do my best work right now.

Monique just relocated to a new town in a new state in November. She took a leave of absence to spend time with her newborn daughter, but now that her daughter is old enough to start preschool, she longs to go back to teaching. She is passionate about teaching and has 18 years of experience in her previous school. She is fortunate to have been hired in December to take over a 2nd grade class for another teacher, Mrs. Garza, who is leaving for maternity leave.

What Monique does not anticipate, however, is that Mrs. Garza is very well-respected by colleagues and loved by her students. From the first day of class, students cannot stop telling her how much they miss their previous teacher. Many of the students struggle to comply with Monique's classroom expectations, and they let her know that Mrs. Garza did not do things the same way. Her colleagues reminisce over how hard Mrs. Garza worked ("Her shoes will be so hard to fill!"). Monique can't help but think, "Hey! Wait a minute! I work hard, too!" She's also experiencing whiplash from all the differences she is encountering compared to her last teaching position—from policy and pay to expectations for after-school duties and lesson plans. She fears that her dream opportunity has become a living nightmare!

*   *   *

Joe is a second-year middle school math teacher in a rural district. He had the great fortune of working on the same teaching team as his mentor, Janna, during his first year. She gave him pointers on class-room management, helped him through all his administrative paper-work, and lent a sympathetic ear when he faced challenges during the school year. Her guidance and friendship have been invaluable to him.

Over the summer, Janna revealed to Joe that she would be taking a new position at another school closer to her home. He congratulated her, but deep inside, he was beginning to panic.

When school begins, Joe immediately faces several challenges. The school has adopted a new math curriculum he feels unprepared to teach. As he is cobbling together lessons each day, he also encounters many persistent student challenges. Many of his newer students seem unprepared for the curriculum he is teaching, and, as a consequence, some of them have begun to act out. Without Janna's presence next door, he is unsure of how best to work with his students, and he doesn't know who he can lean on for support.

Never having worked one-on-one with a coach before, Joe reaches out for a meeting. He discloses to the coach that the changes he didn't anticipate are causing chaos for him and his students. He wants to achieve some sort of equilibrium in his teaching again, but he isn't sure what he needs to do.

✳   ✳   ✳

One of the toughest challenges teachers can experience is disruption. It's like having the rug pulled out from under you. You lose footing, and solid ground betrays you.

Disruptions to our plans can take many forms: classroom man-agement struggles, assignment changes, new administrators, or the departure of trusted colleagues. In 2020, an overwhelming majority of teachers experienced the disruption of the coronavirus pandemic, which resulted in emergency remote teaching—a global shift in instructional delivery. Every disruption causes a rift in what may previ-ously have been a reliable bedrock to our work.

And yet, despite the headaches, disruption can also present opportunities. When we coach an educator through disruption, we can focus on the Compassionate Coaching Focus of Routines. Helping educators gain a more solid foundation of routines can serve them well in the future even as they seek to surmount immediate challenges. Thriving through disruption is about cultivating routines for students, teachers, and coaches so all parties feel like they have established processes to do their best work.

Types of Disruption

We have identified four recurring types of disruption educators experience: classroom, curricular, position, and instructional delivery:

- *Classroom disruption* occurs when the learning environment itself is chaotic. Many issues can contribute to this. For example, in the vignette at the start of this chapter, Joe faces classroom disruption when his students turn to avoidance behaviors because they don't understand his lessons.
- *Curricular disruption* refers to the instructional struggles of changing standards or curriculum materials. Most experienced educators are painfully familiar with the intensity of learning new standards while in the process of implementing them. Joe's active struggles with the school's new curriculum partially contribute to some of the engagement and behavior issues he is seeing.
- *Position disruption* can occur in one of two ways. Educators may change positions in their school, such as going from teaching science to teaching math or from teaching to coaching, or an educator may be in a new school, such as in the case of Monique in the beginning vignette. Monique also has the additional burden of stepping into the role of a beloved teacher to whom she's being constantly compared.
- *Instructional delivery disruption* refers to shifts in how a class is taught. Probably the most common example is a shift from

in-person learning to online learning, but this could also mean a change to school schedules that shortens or lengthens the duration of the class.

All four types of disruption cause similar stresses to educators, leading to less effective learning environments. Not only that, but disruptions can also fuel one another.

One of the most effective actions an educator can take when facing disruption is to focus on establishing or continuing the use of routines. Setting up routines can help create organization out of chaos, easing anxiety and increasing confidence and comfort in the learning process for teachers and students alike. Routines also help lessen the cognitive load of teachers' already demanding tasks, and they are a powerful way to help all parties increase their sense of competence by giving "participants opportunities to be effective across a variety of contexts and to strengthen intra- and inter-personal skills during the school day, in out-of-school-time experiences, or at work" (Hurley et al., 2019, p. 7).

Think about how each of the following strategies can support the teachers with whom you collaborate, and use these ideas as springboards in your coaching conversations.

Implementing Successful Instructional Habits and Routines

Kathy Bonyun, a high school literacy coach in Asheville, North Carolina, remarked to us that a lack of routines is a great source of teacher exhaustion. As she put it, when teachers don't use routines, they "have to be the managers and taskmasters for every one of their kids—individually and on demand—and they don't realize it." In many cases, not only are the teachers' constant explanations and frustrations exhausting for them, they also serve to make the environment even more disruptive as students repeatedly ask clarifying questions about the lesson or turn to avoidance behaviors. These issues are magnified all the more in the case of remote learning, where immediate feedback can't be used as effectively to intervene.

Eric Jensen (2013) explains the importance of habits and routines to those experiencing disruption like this: "When a person is confronted with an adverse situation or a person feels limited control to manage it, his or her brain feels stress. Thus, it makes sense that students who are accustomed to poverty or adverse circumstances have developed certain coping skills to strengthen their locus of control: if they sense their world getting out of control, they may show anger, helplessness, or both" (p. 74). Routines can alleviate some of students' stress and give them a sense of control over their learning.

It will take practice for students to learn routines. However, once they do, they are usually able to dig deeper into the content. Coaches can offer the following resources to teachers to establish different types of routines during times of disruption:

- The Stanford University Graduate School of Education offers routines designed to support students' conceptual math knowledge, mathematical language, and eventual autonomy in group discussions here: https://ell.stanford.edu/sites/default/files/u6232/ULSCALE_ToA_Principles_MLRs__Final_v2.0_030217.pdf
- Douglas Fisher and Nancy Fry offer productive group work routines designed to support personal responsibility, respectful discourse, and collaborative problem solving here: https://dpi.wi.gov/sites/default/files/imce/ela/resources/Fisher_and_Frey_-_Engaging_the_Adolescent_Learner.pdf
- The School Reform Initiative offers protocols for youth engagement to support focused, productive conversations and build collective understanding. You can find more information here: www.schoolreforminitiative.org/protocols-for-youth-engagement
- You can download a weekly reading practice routine from Katie Key Thomas and Jody Guarino that is designed to support expression, accuracy, and prosody (with options for in-person and remote learning) here: https://achievethecore.org/page/3259/weekly-reading-practice-routine

SEL Practices as Instructional Routines

Mary Hurley and colleagues (2019) outline three specific social-emotional learning practices that can function as instructional routines while also supporting positive student-teacher relationships: welcoming/inclusion activities, engaging strategies, and optimistic closure.

Welcoming/inclusion activities. These kinds of activities help students connect with one another and with the teacher while also orienting them for the day's learning. According to Hurley and colleagues (2019), welcoming routines "include a well-taught system of actions or tasks that contribute to an expected rhythm that starts an event. This might be a list of pictures and/or written directions near the door of an elementary classroom, or a 'Do Now' on the board for secondary students that spells out expectations upon arrival.… Practicing these steps… is an investment in creating a calm, orderly space in which learners move with confidence and agency" (p. 10). These routines can include rituals that illustrate to students the importance of building community with one another, such as emoji polls ("Which emoji best represents how you are feeling today?"), choice polls ("Which food has to go?"), or "What's New?" activities (students pair up to share something new in their lives).

Engaging strategies. These are routines that have students engage with one another and the content in productive ways. Most of the routines discussed so far in this chapter fit this category, as do systematic activities such as jigsaw reading and gallery walks. Brain breaks, too, can be included in the repertoire of strategies.

Optimistic closures. These routines can help students summarize their learning, provide them with an opportunity to set goals, and build student agency while also increasing their commitment to learning activities. Here are a few examples:

- *Appreciation, Apology, or Aha!* Students share their appreciation for another student, apologize for a mistake, and share an "aha!" or realization from the lesson (Edutopia, 2018).

- *My Next Step.* Students reflect on what their personal next steps are in the learning process. They can write their reflections on a sticky note or Padlet to reference for the next day's lesson (Hurley et al., 2019).
- *Expressive Go-Round.* Each student responds to the following prompt: "Use one word to describe how you feel about your learning today."

Structured Planning

For some teachers, a new approach to planning itself can make a significant impact on stabilizing the learning environment. Helping teachers examine their lesson-planning structures is essential—especially when they have experienced disruption to instructional delivery, such as switching to remote or hybrid learning. Lesson structures that are transparent and logical benefit teachers by streamlining the planning process. They also support students who benefit from having a clear understanding of lesson goals, activities, and assessments.

We are fans of learning targets as a vehicle for this work. As Sweeney and Harris (2017) share, "When standards-based learning targets are clearly defined at the beginning of the coaching cycle, both the coach and teacher have a road map for the learning opportunities that will be planned over time. Ultimately, these learning targets will provide the criteria by which the teacher, coach, and students will measure their progress toward meeting the goal" (p. 26). Regardless of the kind of disruption a teacher is experiencing, learning targets are critical for effective classroom-based coaching cycles. Collaborating on developing these targets can be a powerful coaching practice that alleviates many pain points. According to Moss and Brookhart (2009), "The single most important method for routinely sharing learning targets is using assignments that match—*really match*—the learning goal" (p. 29). Learning targets also let students envision the outcome of a lesson, enhancing their motivation.

Kenny has worked with teacher leaders and administrators at a high school to develop criteria for assessing the quality of their learning targets. We recommend that coaches use the SMART goal framing to assist teachers in developing similar criteria by asking the following questions:

- Specific
  - Do the targets focus on "chunks" of learning that would happen in one or two class periods?
  - Are the targets written in student-friendly language?
  - Do the targets align with the rigor of the standard?
- Measurable
  - Is there a formative assessment in place to determine which students have met the target?
  - Do the targets include words that can be measured? (Sometimes targets with words like *understand* or *know* can be vague.)
- Attainable
  - Can the target be met in the time allotted?
  - Are the targets ordered in a scaffolded sequence?
- Realistic
  - Can this target realistically be met in the expected amount of time with this group of students?
- Timely
  - Is this target the next logical step based upon what students have already learned?

If a teacher laments that students don't engage with the learning targets, here are some questions the coach can ask him or her to consider:

- Has the teacher clearly defined and unpacked the language of the learning targets?
- Do students have easy access to the learning targets?

- Does the teacher explain to students how the targets assist the learning process?
- Are the targets high-quality (using the above criteria)?
- Do the teacher and students formatively assess their mastery of the targets throughout the learning process?

Types of Planning Structures

Lesson planning can be structured in a variety of ways, depending on the teacher's preferred instructional methods. For example, teachers who use project-based learning tend to plan across several days or weeks rather than day to day. Other teachers use a fixed weekly schedule for some of their class learning activities. For example, an English language arts teacher might choose to focus on self-selected reading on Mondays and Tuesdays, vocabulary building on Wednesdays and Thursdays, and writing concepts on Fridays. These fixed days create a rhythm that helps students feel confident and ready for learning. Teachers do not have to commit a whole class period to these activities, but they may design the first 10 to 20 minutes in a way that grounds students while helping them practice recurring skills.

In the era of remote learning, teachers have found success using daily, weekly, or task-oriented lesson models. For example, several teachers have been able to adapt lesson templates from the popular Hyperdocs site (hyperdocs.co). Using these document-based lessons helps teachers make assignments clear for students. The directions are written and presented in an organized and eye-pleasing way. Several templates already exist, and they all can be easily adapted or integrated into Google Classroom.

Collaborating to Structure Planning

When Kenny's school district abruptly switched to remote learning, he and other district coaches presented weekly virtual workshops where they shared lesson models. He also had other teacher leaders in the district share model lesson planning formats. One excellent coaching strategy is to collect lesson planning models that work well for other teachers, as these have been tested and refined in the proverbial trenches.

One blessing of remote learning is that it enables a greater cross-pollination of ideas between teachers in different schools. As his district turned to remote work, Kenny began to host a weekly one-hour virtual conference with teams from his three schools. To ensure that these meetings were effective and ran smoothly, he created and stuck to the following simple protocol:

1. Check-in. Share how you are doing right now. (first 10 minutes)
2. What successes are you having? (flexible timing based on participants' sharing)
3. What challenges are you facing for which you'd like suggestions? (flexible timing based on participants' sharing)
4. What is one goal you have after our discussion? (last 10 minutes; everyone shares)

This simple protocol created a structured space for teachers to reflect and collaborate. Though it's not a formal coaching cycle, the group reflection meetings did ask teachers to set goals. Facilitating coaches could offer to stay on the call when the meeting is over to see if any teachers want to pursue a coaching cycle with a goal they set for themselves.

Routines to Meet Social-Emotional Needs

Shelly Pratt, an instructional coach and certified yoga instructor in Sioux City, Iowa, brought her two areas of expertise together when she developed "Mindful Monday." She started this routine as a way to help students with social and emotional regulation, but she was thinking of teachers' needs as well. Each Monday morning at 8:45, Shelly used the school intercom to lead mindfulness activities for the whole elementary school. Sometimes she did breathwork or introduced a new breathing activity, such as volcano breath or five-finger breath. Other days, she read a meditation story. Mondays soon became everyone's favorite day, including the teachers. Shelly knew firsthand that teaching can be a stressful job, and she was grateful to notice the staff seemed calmer, happier, and less stressed following the implementation of Mindful Mondays.

We've noticed more and more instructional coaches focusing on the social and emotional needs of teachers. For some, this means organizing an after-school exercise or yoga group. For others, it means supplying a few stress-reducing resources in a newsletter. Here are a few of our favorite free resources coaches can use to support teachers facing disruption:

- **Headspace for Educators** (headspace.com/educators): This app features guided meditations that can be used with both adults and students. Headspace offers free access to all K–12 teachers, school administrators, and supporting staff in the United States, United Kingdom, Canada, and Australia.
- **Yoga with Adriene** (yogawithadriene.com): Adriene provides numerous free yoga workouts on YouTube that can be accessed through her website.
- **Insight Timer** (insighttimer.com): This is the world's largest collection of free guided meditations, featuring over 55,000 titles.
- **HASfit** (hasfit.com): This website offers access to numerous free workouts.
- **UCLA Mindful** (uclahealth.org/ucla-mindful): This easy-to-use app from UCLA's Mindful Awareness Research Center lets you practice guided mindfulness meditation anywhere, anytime.

Sometimes teachers just need to have a safe space to gather and bond with one another. When Kathy coached at an elementary school, she would occasionally set up a coffee bar in the staff lounge—particularly during times of heightened stress, such as the week of parent-teacher conferences. "Coffee with a Coach" was a big draw, and Kathy noticed a sense of calm and joy among attendees.

Implementing Routines in Coaching Work

Many of the strategies we mentioned above are helpful to coaches, too! SEL strategies, planning structures, and coaching routines can also help you through disruption. However, we wanted to offer guidance on two of the biggest disruptions we hear coaches mention: dealing with their inbox and keeping meetings on track.

Creating an Email Routine

Creating an email routine allows us to get—and stay—on top of the never-ending nightmare that email can present. One idea is to set designated times during the school day to check email. Many have found that first thing in the morning and last thing in the afternoon are *not* the best times. When we check email first thing, it can set the course for our day and, sometimes, can lead us astray from our goals. When we check at the end of the day, we are prolonging our time at school and possibly rushing to get through it all. Instead, try mid-morning and right after lunch.

If you don't have a set email routine in place, try to adhere to one for at least two weeks. Reflect on your own or with your own coach on what you are noticing as you tame the email monster.

Using Protocols for Complex Processes

A protocol is a clearly defined routine designed to investigate information to arrive at a deeper understanding of it. Many protocols also end with sharing action steps. During times of disruption, they can serve as helpful routines. Most have specific steps to follow through the process. Many protocols even set the same expectations and "airtime" for talking for everyone. As Kathy Bonyun says, "They draw out people who might otherwise be drowned out."

If your team meetings have gone awry, adding a protocol to guide complex discussions may just save your sanity. One of our most used sites is the National School Reform Faculty (available at https://nsrfharmony.org/protocols), where you will find more than 200 protocols designed to guide discussions, data analysis, team building, and more.

*   *   *

Take the time to think through how the Compassionate Coaching Focus of Routines can help you support teachers as they struggle through classroom, curriculum, position, and instructional delivery disruptions. Although disruptions are inevitable, routines let us create order out of chaos and build systems that support students, teachers, and schools.

6

Coaching Through Isolation

I don't have the community to do my best work right now.

Mike is ecstatic because of his new teaching position. He has been hired as the robotics teacher in a new STEAM high school. In his previous position, he taught drafting to middle schoolers. His new school will be using the project-based learning model, which is not something he knows well yet.

When Mike starts the year, his students are positive and excited to be in his classes, but he does not yet have a clear picture of how to shape his classes to best serve them. He has been provided with a curriculum from the state's education department, but he finds that sometimes the lessons go awry because he doesn't understand some of the robotics content. He wishes he could brainstorm with someone to help him feel more prepared for his classes, but he doesn't know who. He is the only robotics teacher within 100 miles of his school.

✳   ✳   ✳

Lynn is a fourth-year high school English teacher who recently changed positions. Previously, she was one of two advanced placement English teachers in her school. She loved having someone to bounce ideas off of and has shared that such collaboration helped her grow as an educator. She always looked forward to the weekly planning meetings with her teaching partner.

This year, Lynn is responsible for the freshman English classes. She has found herself working with a new team of teachers who have worked together for several years. She feels comfortable with the content, but she feels like she could learn more about working with younger teens. In addition, her new team has shared curriculum and pacing guides with her, but she feels that she doesn't understand all the logistics and purposes behind each lesson. Since her colleagues are used to the curriculum and grade level, Lynn doesn't feel like they share her needs. She fears some of her questions might make her look incompetent to her new peers and doesn't know how to connect with and learn from a team that, by all appearances, functions as a well-oiled machine.

✳   ✳   ✳

Many teachers feel a sense of isolation, both in small and large school settings. As classroom teachers, we both recall sometimes going for days without adult conversations. Teachers get to school and go straight to their classrooms. The bell rings and students arrive. They do have a few breaks, but during that time they are either planning for the next portion of the day or taking care of a few of their own needs. Then there are more specific reasons for feeling isolated. Sometimes a teacher is the only one in the school for a particular grade level or subject matter. (We refer to these teachers as "singletons.") Other teachers may feel isolated because they are brand new in the building and have a hard time fitting into the school culture. On top of that, many teachers work in virtual settings, so they are *literally* isolated.

Isolation can be due to either external conditions or internal psychological states. Consider the vignettes at the start of this chapter. In Mike's case, external conditions keep him feeling isolated, whereas in Lynn's case, the isolation is due to her own worries about not fitting in. Unfortunately, U.S. schools were designed to encourage both forms of isolation. In the early days, one-room schoolhouses were the norm, with one teacher serving all the students and no one with whom to collaborate. Then, as schools grew bigger, teachers were compartmentalized within buildings and grade levels, with little time to collaborate with one another.

Studies show that new teachers are much more likely to stay in the profession if they have a mentor with whom they work closely and if they have time to collaborate with other teachers, especially in the same subject area (Ingersoll, 2012), and that student achievement improves when educators work together (Ostovar-Nameghi & Sheikhahmadi, 2016). What's more, people who lack close social connections are more likely to die prematurely and be negatively affected by stressful events (Myers, 2000). Therefore, helping teachers collaborate and feel a sense of connection is also important for their physical health.

The Compassionate Coaching Focus of Connection is an important goal when supporting teachers who are either physically or psychologically isolated. Here, we share some ideas and strategies that can be implemented in your coaching work.

Encouraging Healthy Relationships

Encouraging teachers to seek out and nurture healthy relationships with one another is an important part of our coaching work. Diener and Seligman (2002) found that having more close social ties makes people happier. Finding ways for isolated teachers to connect with colleagues in both formal and informal environments can make a huge difference in their job satisfaction, outlooks on their students, and teaching efficacy.

Promoting Trust

Building trust is an essential component of coaching others. As coaches who are trying to connect teachers, we must also open spaces for teachers to build trust with one another.

We must become models of how to show vulnerability so others see that it is okay for us to be open with one another and that vulnerability is a preferred pathway to become a closer and stronger team. We are inspired by the words of social scientist Brené Brown (2019):

True belonging requires us to believe in and belong to ourselves so fully that we can find sacredness both in being a part of something and in standing alone when necessary. But in a culture that's rife with perfectionism and pleasing, and with the erosion of civility, it's easy to stay quiet, hide in our ideological bunkers, or fit in rather than show up as our true selves and brave the wilderness of uncertainty and criticism. But true belonging is not something we negotiate or accomplish with others; it's a daily practice that demands integrity and authenticity. It's a personal commitment that we carry in our hearts. (pp. 40–41)

We strive for this level of personal commitment daily, knowing that it is not easy and takes a lot of practice.

Nurturing Collaborative Structures

Research by Diener and Seligman (2002) shows that social experiences are beneficial to well-being whether they arise naturally or if participants are expected to engage in them. Indeed, Ostovar-Nameghi and Sheikhahmadi (2016) have found that teachers feel empowered by democratized collaboration. The most widely used kinds of democratic collaboration in schools are professional learning communities, professional learning networks, and teacher study groups.

Professional Learning Communities

According to DuFour and Eaker (1998), professional learning communities, or PLCs, share the following characteristics: (1) a shared mission, vision, and values; (2) collective inquiry; (3) collaborative teams; (4) action orientation and experimentation; (5) continuous improvement; and (6) a results orientation. In medium and large schools, PLCs are formed by groups of teachers who share the same grade levels or content courses. Since these groups share the same academic standards, they can more easily create common assessments to learn from students' progress. However, many teachers are singletons, so forming content-focused PLCs within their buildings is impossible.

Helping "Singletons" Create Virtual PLCs

Many of you may support what we refer to as "singleton" teachers—those who are alone in teaching their subject at a school. Teachers in this position may find it helpful to connect remotely with others who teach the same subject via virtual PLCs. These PLCs focus on sharing and developing lessons and assessments or discussing the content area's standards and the best ways to teach those standards.

Coaches and teachers can contact neighboring districts to see if any teachers would like to work together in a virtual PLC. Then, during meetings via Zoom, Google Meet, or some other platform, the teachers can share links to their assessments, learning targets, and classroom activities for discussion. Some districts have early-release days built into their calendars for PLC time. When distances aren't too far, virtual PLCs can sometimes meet in real life on these days.

Professional Learning Networks

Professional learning networks, or PLNs, are loose connections among peers on social media platforms such as Facebook, Instagram, or Twitter. These networks can be used to learn either professional or personal skills and knowledge. They illustrate Siemens and Downes's educational theory of *connectivism*, which can be described as "learners creating their own connections and developing a network that goes beyond the people they interact with on a regular basis and which can include people they have never met personally or will ever meet in person" (National Council of Teachers of English, 2016, para. 4).

One way that PLNs can be advantageous is by offering "just-in-time" support for teachers. As a teacher, Ben Owens discovered the #BFC530 "breakfast chat" on Twitter—perfect for an early riser like Ben. The chat occurs each weekday from 5:30 to 5:45 a.m., and each one features a single question for discussion. "Slow-chatting," or engaging in discussion at any time during the day using the #BFC530 hashtag, is also highly encouraged. Ben found that he would often wake up anxious about the lessons he had planned for the day, turn to the #BFC530 chat for advice, and field five or six potential solutions within minutes.

Popular Twitter Hashtags for Educators

In addition to #BFC530, there is an abundance of hashtags on Twitter designed specifically for educators. Here is just a sampling of some that may be useful to you:

- **#BookCampPD:** Book Camp PD is an online group of educators who read professional books and discuss them together (see their website at bookcamppd.com/summer-learning). Most chats occur on Sundays at 7:30 p.m. EST.
- **#DisruptTexts:** Disrupt Texts is a movement to rebuild the literary canon using an antibias, antiracist critical literacy approach. The #DisruptTexts slow chat takes place each week on Twitter using a question posted on Monday at 8:00 a.m EST.
- **#EduColor:** EduColor seeks to elevate the voices of public school advocates of color regarding issues of educational equity and justice. The chat occurs the last Thursday of every month from 7:30 to 8:30 p.m. EST.
- **#edugladiators:** EduGladiators focuses on leadership, engagement, and advocacy based on what is best for kids. The chat occurs on Saturdays at 9:00 a.m. EST.
- **#g2great:** The Good to Great chat is dedicated to continuing the conversation about teacher reflection. The name comes from Mary Howard's book *Good to Great Teaching*. Chats occur on Thursdays at 7:30 p.m. EST.
- **#langchat:** This hashtag supports discussion and free professional learning for world language teachers. Chats occur on Thursdays at 8:00 p.m. EST.
- **#LeadUpChat:** A weekly chat to further the conversations about leadership, culture, growth, and change. Chats occur on Saturdays at 9:30 a.m. EST.

- **#MTBoS:** MTBoS is an acronym for "Math Twitter Blog-o-Sphere." The community is for math teachers who blog or tweet. It is an ongoing conversation sharing ideas and resources. Learn more at mathtwitterblogosphere.weebly.com.
- **#pd4uandme:** This chat occurs every Saturday at 8:30 a.m. EST and focuses on one question related to professional development.
- **#satchat:** This weekly Twitter discussion for current and emerging school leaders takes place Saturdays at 8 a.m. EST. Learn more at www.evolvingeducators.com/satchat-topic.html.
- **#tlap:** Teach Like a Pirate is a weekly chat for educators who embrace Dave Burgess's approach to education as detailed in his *Teach Like a Pirate* book and other books from his publishing company. Chats occur on Mondays at 9 p.m. EST.

Teacher Study Groups

Teacher study groups are teams of educators that voluntarily collaborate on professional learning. These are usually small, formal groups that use protocols to discuss professional readings, brainstorm solutions to problems, analyze student work, or observe one another. Ostovar-Nameghi and Sheikhahmadi (2016) note that such groups, which "get together to present the teaching problems they sense, stating them, and finally solving them through collaborative reflection and discussion [are] an efficient alternative to the once popular teacher training courses, where teachers were at the consumer end of the initiatives" (p. 202). These groups can differ from PLCs in that they do not have to focus on the same standards or outcomes and their work may not follow the same sequence.

Virtual Coaching Cohorts

Virtual coaching cohorts are an excellent way to have teachers work together on a specific topic over a fixed period. A coaching cohort is similar to an online class in that it has a curricular sequence and individual assignments. However, it differs in that teachers have some control over the pacing of assignments. They also sometimes have choice over which assignments they will complete, and they receive individualized or group coaching at certain checkpoints in their learning.

Kenny facilitated a virtual coaching cohort on writing from sources through Google Classroom. The teachers who participated self-enrolled in the course because they wanted to learn new ways to teach evidence-based writing. After reading an introductory blog post on writing from sources that Kenny assigned, teachers were able to research areas of focus for evidence-based writing using a choice board. (Figure 6.1 shows the assignments teachers completed for each of these areas, noting where teachers received individualized coaching as well.)

Creating Norms for Collaboration

Norms are an important yet often overlooked precursor to effective collaboration. Frustrations in meetings often stem from lack of clarity about the processes or goals, participants lacking ways to share their voice, or roles being assigned regardless of people's areas of strength. Norms offer agreed-upon ways for group members to collaborate better in meetings. In short-term situations, such as workshops, a facilitator can write the norms, share them with the group, and then seek additional norms or revisions to the existing ones. However, for longer-term commitments such as PLCs or teacher study groups, setting aside time early on for team members to develop norms together can help the group feel much more satisfied with its work.

Norms do not need to be too complicated, and most groups work best with no more than six norms in place (and no fewer than three). Here, for instance, are the norms for a group of high school English language arts teachers who met as a PLC on Friday mornings:

- We set a goal to work toward for every meeting at the previous meeting.

- We commit to learn from one another.
- We focus on solutions.
- We are flexible with start time.

FIGURE 6.1 **Writing from Sources Cohort**	
Virtual Group Assignments	**Individual Coaching**
1. "Designing High-Quality Writing Tasks" blog and discussion board	
2. Read through the writing research choice board.	
	3. Coach works with each participant to identify a meaningful writing goal based on their students' next steps.
4. Select a writing professional development focus and create an implementation plan (which guides coaching). Share goal with colleagues to seek out potential partnerships.	
	5. Coach meets with each teacher and offers support through the implementation plan via coaching conversations, resource ideas, co-planning, or co-teaching.
6. Reflect on the successes of the selected writing strategy, and share the outcomes with one another.	

These norms communicate the tone of the PLC and recognize team members' needs (e.g., by offering flexible start times). One of our favorite ways to begin creating norms is by following Daniel Venables's Peeves and Traits protocol (Venables, 2011). The protocol is simple. Participants are each given an index card and asked to write one pet peeve they have about working in groups. After a few minutes, everyone flips over the card to write one trait that makes them a good collaborator. Then participants share for about 10 minutes, which can lead to both funny and eye-opening conversations. Coaches or other leaders facilitating use of this protocol can help the team discover patterns and roles that might guide them to work effectively together.

Another simple method for creating norms is affinity mapping, a quick and efficient way to find consensus in a group. For example, imagine that two teachers will be co-teaching together for the first time. The teachers separately think through and jot down procedures and routines and how they want students to feel during the lesson, then they compare what they've written and use any similarities to develop their norms for working together. In large groups, teachers can post their ideas, then assign a volunteer to organize like ideas. The largest clumps of similar ideas then form the starting point for developing collaborative norms.

Coordinate and Support Low-Stakes Classroom Visits

According to research by Steve Barkley (2016), only 7 percent of U.S. teachers say that their school has a strong collaborative model, and more than 50 percent claim never to have seen a colleague teacher. Nevertheless, the benefits of teachers working together and watching one another in action are countless. Even "singleton" teachers can learn something by observing a colleague who teaches a different subject. In large school buildings or campuses, teachers can interact with peers with whom they don't often collaborate. Many teachers have learned a great deal not only by seeing other teachers teach but also by watching their students excel in other classrooms.

Here we offer a few approaches teachers can use to conduct low-stakes classroom visits. We encourage you to explore these ideas on your own and watch for opportunities in your school to plant the seeds with teachers by discussing these structures with them. The informal, low-stakes nature of these approaches is intended to encourage building connections.

"Matchmaker" Month

Middle school literacy coach Rebecca Johnson and high school literacy coach Laura Mayer developed a Matchmaker activity in their schools. The idea began when the two of them collaborated to brainstorm new ways of approaching public teaching. Both had previously conducted public teaching activities like learning walks, but they wanted to develop a way to personalize this type of professional learning for individual teachers.

Many of Rebecca and Laura's teachers had expressed interest in a deeply focused and personalized opportunity to observe a colleague. In late January, they promoted a "Matchmaker" process in their schools to occur in February (inspired by Valentine's Day, of course). They asked teachers to respond to a Google Form asking them about strengths of theirs that they would be willing to share. The form also asked them about any areas of practice they would like to strengthen.

After collecting the responses, Rebecca and Laura began organizing teachers into observer-host pairs. The observers reached out to the hosts to find a class period during the month in which they could observe a practice they wanted to strengthen. Of course, based on their responses, some teachers found themselves in two pairs, when the person they observed did not necessarily need to learn the strength they planned to share. Most collaborations occurred within the school, although some happened across schools. Teachers had until the end of February to conduct their visits and complete a reflection on the process. Some teachers learned new ideas from colleagues they had barely met before. Subject areas and grade levels intermingled in most of the matches as well.

Laura shared one anecdote about an intensive intervention teacher (a "singleton") who visited another intensive intervention teacher at a sister high school. She learned about how the teacher used an "accountabiliTREE" with speaking "stems" to help her students with discussions and interactions in the classroom. Laura noted that the observing teacher met with the host teacher to get ideas and resources, and, by the next week, she and her students were using their own "accountabiliTREE" for their class discourse. The teacher continued to meet with Laura as they co-planned ways to use the tree for different classroom activities.

Kenny also used the Matchmaker idea in his schools, and after surveying participants, he found that whereas 90 percent of observers stated that the visits were beneficial to their teaching practice, only 40 percent of hosts said the same. However, in their descriptive commentaries, most teachers discussed how they had connected with one another *following* the visits. Here are just a few samples of what they said:

- "Working with Mrs. D, I was able to learn some great strategies for project-based learning, self-evaluation, peer evaluation, and goal setting."
- "I was able to reflect with Mr. R about why I do some of the things I do, which reminds me of some of the things I leave out and don't intentionally teach enough."
- "Observing the chorus class helped me think of new roles for my students in group work and made me realize how students can be responsible leaders. The host talked with me, which helped me realize that if I stay true to group processes, I can also create growth in my readers."

Pineapple Charts

Another informal way to have teachers share their expertise is the pineapple chart. Teachers use this document, named after the famous symbol of hospitality, to invite one another to visit their classrooms to see lessons or practices in action. Teachers add their names to class periods when others are invited to see them teach. They also include a strategy or lesson topic that they have students working on during that class period. The chart can also be printed out and posted in a common area of the school. (See Figure 6.2 for an example of a pineapple chart.)

FIGURE 6.2
Sample Pineapple Chart

	Monday	Tuesday	Wednesday	Thursday	Friday
1st block	Chen Vocabulary Relay				Palmer Digital Breakout
2nd Block		Ramirez Mock City Council	Ramirez Mock City Council		Palmer Digital Breakout
Smart Lunch/ Clubs			George Socratic Seminar with Book Club		
3rd Block	Chen Vocabulary Relay				Palmer Digital Breakout
4th Block			Laurie Key Features Lesson	Laurie Key Features Lesson	

Summer Pettigrew, an elementary school teacher in South Carolina, helped facilitate pineapple charts in her school when she was a coach there. She found that the charts helped democratize the sharing of expertise and widened the pool of professional learning connections teachers could make in their school. "It's typical that the same few teachers are highlighted, and we wanted everyone to feel they had something to bring to the table," she told us. "The idea is that you pop in for a very informal 10 to 15 minutes to look for something specific—not to critique." She went on to tell us that one benefit of the chart for teachers is the ability to collaborate with people they may not usually see in the school.

One issue with pineapple charts and other informal visits is that teachers might not be able to visit or host colleagues who have the same planning times. In some schools, other teachers, administrators, coaches, or floating substitute teachers will cover classes for a specific amount of time for this purpose. When teachers sign up on the pineapple chart, they can also list a specific time, such as "10:30 to 11:00" or "the first 15 minutes of class," to help teachers schedule coverage.

Forming Connections as a Coach

Coaches are often isolated in their work as well. A single coach may be the only educator in that position in a school—or sometimes in multiple schools. Coaches also benefit from connections with other coaches in order to improve their effectiveness and satisfaction in their roles.

Are there other instructional coaches in your district or neighboring districts? If so, reach out to them to form local network groups. Try checking with your administrator to see if you could meet other instructional coaches in the area for a few hours once a month. Perhaps you could alternate the schools that hold these networking meetings so each host could highlight specific work they are doing. Are there events where coaches gather? Are there ways to leverage technology to connect virtually? Here are some of the best ways for coaches to meet their own connection needs.

Book Studies

Book studies can be a great way for coaches to learn together and help one another implement new ideas into their coaching repertoires.

Coaches can select from the wealth of coaching resources out there and develop a reading schedule, either by reading the whole book and then discussing or by breaking the book into small chunks for discussion. Before the reading starts, group members should articulate what they hope to gain from the series, agree on whether and what kind of facilitation or protocols will be used, and discuss whether they are to implement ideas they read about or debrief experiences together.

Participant-Led Gatherings

These kinds of gatherings go by many names—Edcamps, unconferences, open spaces—but are all designed in a similar way. Participants meet in a given location (such as a school) either on a weekend or as part of a regional networking session, and they proceed to generate topics for breakout sessions, with each participant given the chance to voice ideas. Though a facilitator may be used, his or her role is primarily to keep the conversations moving. Once topics are generated, they are organized into a schedule for the day (see Figure 6.3). The length and number of sessions will vary from event to event; once sessions are organized, participants are free to choose the sessions they attend.

FIGURE 6.3 **Sample Open Space Schedule**					
8:30–9:00	Room	9:00–10:00	10:05–11:05	11:10–12:10	Break for Lunch
Welcome and development of sessions	ROOM A				
	ROOM B				
	ROOM C				
	ROOM D				

When Kathy worked for a regional service agency, she helped build these kinds of gatherings into the agency's monthly sessions throughout the school year, with 30 minutes to an hour of each full day's agenda devoted to them. Approximately six topic areas were typically generated. Within the 60 minutes, participants chose to attend two 30-minute discussions from the generated topics. When the breakout sessions met, chart paper was placed in each area so groups could take notes together and share favorite related resources. Participants were also encouraged to share email addresses to stay in touch if follow-up was needed.

Edcamps can be found in most regions of the United States and 45 other nations around the world (Edcamp Foundation, n.d.). Two South Carolina instructional coaches, Pam Hubler and Allison Walker, have both experienced the tangible benefits of connecting through these kinds of participant-led gatherings. After experiencing the power of connection that Edcamps supply firsthand, they joined colleagues to organize Edcamp South Carolina, where many sessions are geared toward instructional coaches and other school leaders. During the COVID-19 crisis, Pam also teamed up with a geographically diverse group of educators to organize Edcamp Remote Learning (#Edcamp-RL). (To learn more about organizing your own Edcamp, visit edcamp. org.)

Coaching Conferences

We know how hard it can be to secure funding to attend conferences. One way to help with the funding dilemma when making proposals to school leaders is to think through your reasons for attending the conference and how the experience will help you in your role. Coaches might also check with the conference organizers to see if there are scholarships available or volunteering perks that might offset some of the expenses. The following conferences are either geared toward instructional coaches or have instructional coach and teacher leader strands:

- **Teaching Learning Coaching Conference:** Hosted by Jim Knight and the Instructional Coaching Group, this conference takes place every fall and is advertised as the largest instructional coaching conference in the world. It's like Woodstock for instructional coaches! More information can be found on the Instructional Coaching Group website: https://instructional-coaching.com.
- **Region 13 Instructional Coaching Conference:** This conference, known as the ICC, debuted in 2017 and has continued to host dynamic thought leaders in Austin, Texas, every July. You can find more information about the ICC and Region 13 on their website: www4.esc13.net/instruction.
- **CoachFest:** This is a two-day conference and retreat, usually held in the Appalachian mountains, for coaches, teachers, and leaders. There are exemplary professional learning sessions coupled with health and wellness sessions, introvert and extrovert breaktime activities, yoga, and meditation. CoachFest is the vision of instructional and life coach Mia Pumo and is organized by Constructive Learning Design. You can learn more at the Constructive Learning Design website: constructivelearningdesign.org.
- **ASCD Annual Conference:** The annual ASCD conference is ASCD's flagship event and occurs each spring in a different location. Information about the annual conference as well as other ASCD conference offerings can be found at www.ascd.org.
- **Learning Forward Annual Conference:** This conference offers an exceptional instructional coaching strand. More information can be found at https://conference.learningforward.org.

Connecting with Coaches on Twitter

We both connect with inspirational instructional coaches and fellow authors and researchers in the field on a daily basis using Twitter.

In fact, without these connections, you would not even be reading this book: We *met* each other through Twitter!

We've previously mentioned the #educoach Twitter chat, which Kathy cofounded in 2011 alongside colleagues Jessica Johnson and Shira Leibowitz. The chat, led now by a team of great moderators, continues to meet each Wednesday at 9:00 p.m. EST. It is topic-driven and addresses a wide array of coaching-related issues. Here are some other Twitter chats that coaches might find useful:

- **#coachcollaborative:** This chat occurs on Sundays at 8:00 p.m. EST and is focused on discussing books about coaching, leadership, and instruction.
- **#EdCoachCB:** The EdCoach Coffee Break is open to all educators. It occurs on the 13th of each month at 9:00 p.m. EST.
- **#tosachat:** This chat occurs on Twitter every Monday at 11:00 p.m. EST and is for teachers on special assignment, including all technology and instructional coaches.

We hope that you will be on the lookout for colleagues who might be experiencing physical and psychological isolation, and that the strategies we have shared as part of the Compassionate Coaching Focus of Connection will have a positive effect. We also hope that you will try a few for yourself.

7

Coaching Through
School Culture Challenges

I don't have the environment to do my best work right now.

Patrick has taught 7th grade social studies in the same public middle school for five years. Though he has enjoyed working there (for the most part), the professional culture has bothered him. He works with two other social studies teachers in his grade level, but they have never collaborated on any lessons. When Patrick is looking for fresh ideas for lessons, his colleagues usually tell him he should just do what he has always done.

Patrick knows there are ways to improve his students' experiences and learning. He also believes his colleagues across the school have skills he could benefit from learning. However, there are no structures in place to learn from them, and he does not feel like he can bring up the idea himself. At least the way he perceives it, everyone seems content with the way things are.

✳   ✳   ✳

Simone has taught in the primary grades for 15 years. Her family moved to their new community a year ago and she felt fortunate to land a 2nd grade job close to her home. In her previous school, she had been on the building leadership team. Her school was quite progressive when it came to technology. She hated to give that up, but she also knew it was one of the reasons her new school had hired her. Upon her arrival, she was asked by the principal if she'd be interested in joining the leadership team. She felt honored and quickly agreed.

She soon realized that the teachers in her new school were reluctant to incorporate new and emerging technology. When she was asked by the principal to share a tool at professional development, many teachers seemed disengaged. The principal asked teachers to report back at the next professional development session on how they used the tool, but no one really had much to say during that portion of the meeting. She started to feel awkward that she was one of just a few that would share. Instead of sharing successes and swapping ideas, Simone begins to retreat from openly discussing professional growth and reflection.

✳   ✳   ✳

As we see it, there are three types of culture challenges that coaches navigate:

1. **Toxic:** These are the cultures that give visitors an uneasy feeling when they walk in the building. In toxic school cultures, coaches may encounter teachers looking away from them in the hallway or even be aggressively confronted by some teachers. A lot of mistrust and resentment tends to exist between educators and leadership. These are likely the most difficult environments to reshape.

2. **Stagnant:** A culture that has grown stagnant feels stuck in time. Instruction may seem nearly identical to what coaches experienced themselves as students. Teachers often feel tied to traditional structures and ideas in stagnant cultures, making it hard to introduce new approaches.

3. **Shifting:** In a shifting culture, a new or outside force has created a pressing need for internal change. For example, say a new principal wants to reenvision the instructional framework of a school. Teachers need to make this shift because their supervisor will evaluate them on their performance on this new framework. Shifting cultures emerge when schools

implement new curricula, scheduling, or instructional formats (such as shifting to remote learning).

To help teachers navigate challenging school cultures, we recommend coaches use the Compassionate Coaching Focus of Openness in their coaching. Goals for this focus area include identifying teacher leaders as potential partners, making teaching public, building collective teacher efficacy, and celebrating successes.

Empowering Teacher Leaders as Partners in Developing a Culture of Coaching

According to Ben Owens, founder and chief innovation officer of Open Way Learning, "seeking out teacher leaders means embracing collective autonomy through a distributed leadership model, where teachers are empowered to bring the best ideas forward to shape the decisions from the classroom level to school policy." Forming a culture of distributed leadership allows teachers to take the lead when their experiences match the needs of the school.

Though there isn't a consensus in the field on how to precisely define *teacher leadership*, the Teacher Leader Model Standards of the Teacher Leadership Exploratory Consortium (TLEC) define it as "the process by which teachers... influence their colleagues, principals, and other members of the school community to improve teaching and learning practices with the aim of increased student learning and achievement" (n.d., p. 10). The first domain of the Teacher Leader Model Standards centers on school culture and calls for "fostering a collaborative culture to support educator development and student learning" (p. 9).

In some districts, a misunderstanding about the nature of coaching means teacher leaders are rarely given the opportunity to coach their colleagues. This is unfortunate, because struggling teachers may view coaches as reserved for "failing" teachers but would happily take advice from colleagues who are excelling. Robust and innovative schools develop a culture of coaching among faculty where teachers coach one another. Schools with healthy distributed leadership models incorporate layers of coaching, including peer coaching. Whether or not someone is officially called a "coach" doesn't matter.

Facilitating Coaching Requests

For teachers who feel uncomfortable reaching out for coaching publicly, Kenny designed a "digital coaching menu" that he sends out at the start of every semester. The menu offers teachers options for when they would like to meet, what they want to focus on, and how they want to collaborate (McKee, 2018). Figure 7.1 shows an example of what a digital coaching menu can look like.

FIGURE 7.1
A Sample Coaching Menu

Welcome to the new semester. I look forward to partnering with all content-area teachers to continue advancing student learning. The following menu is a way for us to communicate. Let me know about any areas in which you would like to partner with me, and I will follow up with you in person or by email.

Email address:

What is your school?

Choose any areas you would like to strengthen in your students:
___ Recognizing what they have learned and still need to learn
___ Participating in small- and large-group discussions
___ Improving performance on standardized or summative assessments
___ Improving engagement
___ Reading in my content area
___ Reading complex texts
___ Writing in my content area
___ Learning new vocabulary
___ Building the content knowledge of my standards
___ Participating in the research process
___ Organizing their thinking and writing
___ Including physical movement in class activities
___ Other:

Please choose the methods of collaboration and learning that work best for you:

____ Coach teaches a strategy in class. Teacher watches and reflects on student learning.

____ Teacher teaches a strategy in class. Coach watches and reflects on student learning.

____ We co-plan a lesson or unit.

____ We co-plan and co-teach a lesson in your class.

____ Coach supports your PLC functionality and goals.

____ We informally discuss topics of your choice and brainstorm next steps.

____ We explore technology tools that support learning/literacy.

____ Coach arranges for colleagues to observe one another or participate in public teaching.

____ We explore student work or assessment data together.

____ Coach assists in developing/finding resources or research.

____ Not sure yet, but the coach can come by to have an informal discussion of options.

____ Other:

Where do you prefer to meet?

What is (are) your content area(s)?

When do you prefer to meet?

____ Before school

____ Planning time

____ After school

____ An early-release day/teacher workday

How soon would you like to work together? This information helps me prioritize scheduling.

____ As soon as possible

____ During this nine-week period

____ During this semester, but how soon is flexible

____ Other:

Source: Copyright Kenny McKee, used with permission.

Making Teaching Public

What we mean when we say teaching should be public is that teachers should open their classrooms to learn from one another and schools should recognize that *instruction is worth studying.*

Teacher leaders can facilitate reflection on and analysis of instruction. As Saphier and West (2009) explain, this "can happen a couple of times a year in small groups, or the coach and lead teachers can include individual teachers as needed in a planning, teaching, reflection cycle throughout the year" (p. 48). In schools with challenging cultures, establishing such a process may take time, but it's still very worthwhile.

Opening classroom doors is a bit like opening a teacher's heart and soul. As Brené Brown (2018) writes,

> We must be guardians of spaces that allow students to breathe, be curious, and to explore the world and be who they are without suffocation. They deserve one place where they can rumble with vulnerability and their hearts can exhale. And what I know from the research is that we should never underestimate the benefit to a child of having a place to belong—even one—where they can take off their armor. It can and often does change the trajectory of their life. (p. 13)

The same holds true for teachers. Developing environments in which teachers are free to breathe, be curious, and explore leads to an atmosphere of shared learning.

As a 5th grade teacher, Kathy implemented literature circles in her classroom. Soon, her colleagues in the school and even in other schools began asking to attend and observe this strategy in action. Toward the end of each observation, she would ask the principal for coverage so she could debrief with the visiting teachers by asking them what they noticed and what questions they had.

Learning Walks

Learning walks are a popular public teaching activity in many schools where teachers observe student learning by visiting colleagues' classes. The extra benefit is that these visits also improve school culture. When setting up learning walks, coaches first need to provide a clear explanation of the purpose for them—usually, they're for teachers to learn more about how students are learning and what instructional moves their colleagues use. A broad purpose such as this can help teachers feel at ease with the process.

Learning walks always work best when the host teachers volunteer to let others visit. For this reason, it's a good idea to let teachers opt in and for them to select the times they think work best for visits, as this creates a sense of ownership in the process while showing teachers that you respect their needs.

We find that a Google Form survey allows us to easily collect the information we need to build a solid learning walks schedule (see Figure 7.2). Coaches should make sure to provide a detailed explanation of the process and ensure that everyone knows the standard meeting place where the walks begin.

When teachers have arrived for their learning walk, they should be provided with a list of questions to think about during the walk and to discuss at the end of the process. Because many teachers are hesitant to take notes during walks, worried that it might seem evaluative to the host teacher, learning walks might need to be short—maybe just 10 to 15 minutes—so participants can recall the details.

Here are some sample learning walk questions we have used in the past:

- What learning activities were students doing?
- What digital learning strategies or tools did we see?
- What was the teacher enabling his/her students to do? What evidence do we have that supports this?
- Were the students getting a deep understanding of the desired learning outcomes? If so, what evidence did we observe?

- What can we take back to our classroom after visiting this classroom?

After, teachers might debrief their learning walk by answering the question "What patterns did you observe across classrooms?"

FIGURE 7.2
Sample Learning Walks Survey

A learning walk is an opportunity for a group of teachers to visit a few classrooms (usually three) and discuss how they see students engaging in different facets of the instructional framework. The visiting teachers discuss evidence of the instructional framework and reflect on how it can influence their practice. A facilitator (instructional coach or fellow teacher) will lead these discussions. Visiting teachers will also leave a note of positive feedback for the host teachers they visit.

What is your planning period (i.e., when you can visit classes)?
____ 1st block
____ 2nd block
____ 3rd block
____ 4th block

Which dates are you able to go on a learning walk? Please check ALL that apply.
____ April 15
____ April 20
____ April 22

Willingness to Be Visited

Our learning walks are an opportunity to learn from one another. We are not looking for staged lessons. We want to see in what ways different teachers are engaging students within the instructional framework. We need several volunteers to make the visits a success, and we would love to visit your class on one or two of the days. You will know which days you will have visitors once the calendar is completed.

Would you be willing to let a few colleagues visit your classes for about 10–15 minutes?
__ Yes
__ No

To support a positive school culture, we also recommend that participants leave a positive note for each teacher they visit about something successful they observed in their classroom. Teachers generally give these to the leader of the walk, who then distributes these kudos to the host teachers' mailboxes. This is an especially good practice for schools new to learning walks, as it helps affirm the value of the process.

Learning walks can be accomplished remotely, too. For example, Kenny uses online videos of teachers employing different vocabulary strategies for discussion on Google Meet. He simply shares his screen and plays the videos between group discussions.

Professional Learning Teams

Once a coach has regularly worked with several teachers in a school, he or she can think about how a professional learning team might be used to improve the school's culture. For example, some schools have literacy leadership teams (LLTs) in place that are responsible for using information from surveys, testing, and other data sources to identify literacy needs in the school, consider potential solutions, and develop a schoolwide plan for literacy-focused professional learning. Pamela Craig (2010) suggests four types of teachers who should be recruited for this type of team: skillful communicators, open-minded diplomats, teachers deeply committed to students, and positive teachers who inspire colleagues. (In our experience, people with these four qualities are options for any professional learning team.)

Dr. Chaunté Garrett has experience recruiting professional learning teams. She noticed that while her beginning teachers were "eating out of the hands" of veteran teachers at the school, they had trouble engaging during professional learning workshops for new teachers. When she was the school head, Chaunté had planned to introduce a set of common teaching strategies for the school, which she realized many of the veteran teachers already used. Therefore, she invited these veteran teachers to a meeting where she introduced the strategies, emphasized that she had seen several of them masterfully using some of them, and asked for their help in spreading these strategies to other teachers in the school.

Chaunté knew that these teacher leaders' views of the instructional strategies would make or break the success of the initiative. The teacher leaders worked alongside her and their curriculum coaches for an hour each week to unpack the strategies and envision how they would best work for their students and how they could best support teachers in using them. She noticed that working alongside the veteran teachers on an equal level helped newer teachers see themselves as leaders and agents of change. They opened their minds to the process, and they developed greater collective efficacy to influence the learning of all the school's students.

Peer Coaching Teams

Early in Kathy's career as an instructional coach, she had the pleasure of learning directly from Beverly Showers and her research on peer coaching—something that made a lasting impact on her work as a coach. Showers and her colleague Bruce Joyce have been instrumental in providing a comprehensive guide to schoolwide renewal, including stimulating cultural changes that transfer learning from the "workshop," or professional learning opportunity, to the "workplace," or day-to-day work. They found that of all the training components they studied, peer coaching had the greatest impact when it came to transferring what was learned into practice. Each component increased educators' knowledge and skill at various levels, but it wasn't until they added coaching with the components of theory, demonstration, practice, and feedback that they saw impressive gains in knowledge (2.71 effect size), skill (1.25), and transfer of training (1.68) (Joyce & Showers, 2002). Clearly, peer coaching (and coaching in general) is powerful.

Kenny worked with Dr. Donna Lanahan, principal of Buncombe County Early and Middle Colleges in Asheville, North Carolina, to create a framework of peer coaching that teachers have found beneficial for their professional growth. Donna worked with her teachers to first develop a schoolwide instructional vision, then to create an instructional feedback tool with eight instructional practice goals. There was just one problem. How do you support eight instructional goals at once? Teachers, administrators, and the coach tried to observe one another and give feedback on too much. Consequently, Donna settled on just one of the goals, engagement, for everyone. Engagement would be the focus of schoolwide professional learning sessions, and it would be a part of any classroom visit. Kenny and Donna then set up peer coaching teams, with each teacher selecting one additional goal as a focus for the semester. Teams of three teachers gave and received feedback to one another according to the following protocols:

- Each teacher received at least one 20- to 45-minute visit from his or her peer coaches approximately once a month.
- The school held weekly teaching and learning meetings with at least 30 minutes reserved for peer coaching teams to meet.
- Paper copies of the instructional feedback tool were made available in the workroom for teachers to use during visits.
- For every visit, a peer coach facilitated a reflective debriefing with the host teacher and other observing teachers.

Kenny provided professional development on coaching conversations, including a script that teachers could use. The teachers also watched videos of lessons on YouTube, and they practiced using the feedback tool. Finally, teachers used a "teacher takeaway form" to share their reflections on the process. Here are a few examples of what they wrote:

- "I need to use engagement activities for listeners during presentations. I will try think-pair-share activities before presentations. I should also have students utilize graphic organizers during the presentation to keep them on topic the entire time, particularly during longer presentations."
- "I tried a new (to me) protocol and had concerns about lag time and staggered finishes. My peers gave great suggestions

for tiered responses to differentiate with the groupings. We also discussed ways to deal with "dominant" voices in the classroom to give voice to others. I think I will revisit the instructional feedback tool to see how I can improve."

- "That the learning targets for the lesson were clear! The students were working on an activity to reinforce and practice an algorithmic skill.... I need to do more debriefing at the end of the lesson or when I switch topics."

The Consultancy Protocol

When Ben Owens worked as a project-based learning teacher at Tri-County Early College in Murphy, North Carolina, he and his colleagues collaborated on schoolwide interdisciplinary and cross-grade projects for which the consultancy protocol came in very handy. Developed by Faith Dunne, Paula Evans, and Gene Thompson-Grove, the Consultancy protocol involves educators presenting their peers with "an issue that raises questions, an idea that seems to have conceptual gaps, or something about process or product that you just can't figure out" (National School Reform Initiative, n.d., p. 1). Educators can use this protocol to keep professional dialogue focused on the educational goal. The full protocol can be found at www.schoolreforminitiative .org/download/consultancy. To engage in the protocol, educators take the following roles: (1) the presenter, a teacher whose work is being discussed by the group; (2) the facilitator, someone who organizes the group, monitors the protocol, and sometimes participates in the discussion; and (3) participants who discuss the dilemma. We highly recommend referring to the full protocol before using it, but here are the six main steps:

1. The presenter gives an overview of the dilemma the group will be discussing, framed as a question to be answered. (10–15 minutes)

2. The group asks clarifying questions of the presenter. (5 minutes)

3. The group asks probing questions of the presenter. (10 minutes)

4. The group discusses the dilemma. (15 minutes)

5. The presenter reflects on what he or she has heard and is thinking. (5 minutes)

6. The facilitator leads a brief conversation about the group's assessment of the effectiveness of the Consultancy process. (5 minutes)

The teachers at Tri-County Early College liked this protocol so much they started using it for topics other than schoolwide projects. For example, teachers with a passion for building community connections would meet to develop better ways to find community partners and navigate barriers between school and community partnerships using the protocol.

Lab Sites

Lauren Smith, instructional coach in Noblesville, Indiana, has found success with student-centered lab sites, which allow educators to bring professional development into the classroom while maintaining a student-centered focus. The coach partners with a classroom teacher, who serves as the lab site host, to support and scaffold a professional learning experience for colleagues and students. Lab sites can occur with as little or as much time as needed, across a single day or multiple days and require no prior preparation from the host (Sweeney, 2011). Lauren was first drawn to student-centered lab sites because they are a good fit if "you are interested in building a collegial school culture" (Sweeney, 2011, p. 114).

Student-centered lab sites follow a structure and discussion protocol (Sweeney, 2011). Prior to entering the lab site, participants engage in a prebriefing where they discuss an overarching focus question and generate relevant look-fors. During the lab site, the coach facilitates a learning experience where the participants first observe a host teacher teaching a classroom lesson. During the classroom observation, participants take notes related to the focus question and look-fors. They may also reflect alongside a student to gather evidence of their learning.

Following the lab site, participants follow a protocol to reflect on the focus question and any look-fors, discuss the learning experience, and determine any further actions. The coach facilitates this process, getting feedback on the experience. Lauren was thrilled to find that this process built the collegial learning culture she was striving for at her school. Through this professional inquiry and iteration of repeated practice, cohorts are able to foster collective teacher efficacy as well as individual growth with the support of colleagues.

Encouraging Collective Teacher Efficacy

One of the most important goals for a coach who is working through school culture challenges is to begin creating a climate of collective teacher efficacy. A shared belief among school staff that student learning can be improved if teachers collectively meet certain goals is "strongly and positively associated with student achievement across subject areas and in multiple locations" (Eells, 2011, p. 110). According to Donohoo (2017), the three conditions necessary to foster collective teacher efficacy are advanced teacher influence, goal consensus, and responsiveness of leadership.

Teacher influence. Providing teachers with a good measure of autonomy and leadership in school decisions is essential (Donohoo, 2017). As Sherri Lewis (2009) states, "With more opportunity to participate in school decision-making, teams build more mastery experiences in this type of decision-making and experience social persuasion through colleagues' feedback" (p. 72). Establishing "dependable, high-trust, collaborative structures" is a high priority for this work (Donohoo, Hattie, & Eells, 2018, p. 42). Many of the public teaching structures we've described in this chapter support the priority of teacher influence.

Goal consensus. Coaching groups of educators to set and reach consensus on meaningful goals is a worthy goal for supporting educators during school culture challenges. Viviane Robinson and colleagues (2009) suggest that, for a group to reach consensus, it should have both the capacity and commitment to meet its goals, which themselves need to be clear and specific. In addition to these conditions of goal consensus, making sure that school leaders celebrate team accomplishments and effects on students are important for keeping educator teams motivated throughout the process (Donohoo, 2017). Drawing clear connections between collective teacher actions and a positive impact on students is critical for sustaining motivation (Donohoo, Hattie, & Eells, 2018).

Responsiveness of leadership. This final criterion is all about supporting the needs and ideas of educators. "Responsiveness requires awareness of situations—the details and undercurrents in the school," writes Donohoo. "Is anything preventing the team from carrying out their duties effectively?" (2017). Identifying ways to respond to issues that affect your teachers is imperative for nurturing collective teacher efficacy. We believe that understanding the barriers your colleagues face and using the Compassionate Coaching Focus areas can help you achieve this type of responsiveness in your coaching.

Celebrating Successes

A popular quote, attributed to Amy Rees Anderson (2015), has gone viral on social media: "A person who feels appreciated will always do more than what is expected." Could it be that people identify with this quote because they *aren't* feeling appreciated? Acknowledging past successes and celebrating current ones doesn't just boost morale; it can have life-changing effects. Celebrating the successes of others contributes to their feelings of self-efficacy and can encourage positive feelings about the school. As Bolman and Deal (2010) so eloquently put it, "Celebration and ceremony, at their best, are antidotes to boredom, cynicism, and burnout. They bring members of a group together, strengthen bonds, and rekindle a sense of a higher calling and noble purpose. In today's environment, myopic obsession with measurement and short-term outcomes too often overshadows the sometimes magical, long-term influence teachers have on students' lives" (p. 113).

When teachers began leading groups in learning walks at one high school, Kenny made "Giraffe Award" certificates to celebrate and acknowledge their leadership. He called it this because the award goes out to those who "stick out their necks" by taking the lead, trying something new, or stepping in to resolve a difficult situation. When one teacher took the initiative to set up reminders about the learning walks for everyone in Google Calendar, Kenny searched online for animals that are known for their organization and created a "Penguin Award" for that person. These awards have a sweet and silly element to them, but they really make a difference in how people feel. To his surprise, teachers often have these awards prominently displayed in their classrooms or offices after these meetings!

Anchoring Your Coaching Work Through School Culture Challenges

We are not going to lie. It can be rough out there. Coaches are leverage points in helping schools find a healthy culture, but it can sometimes feel like impossible work. Here are a few strategies you can use to help build your own confidence when it is lacking. Let's look at some ways you can persevere while using the Compassionate Coaching Focus of Openness for yourself.

Dealing with Negative Reactions to Coaching

One time, after being told that Kenny was a coach, a teacher remarked that he was "a waste of a salary." Ouch! Even though negative reactions can sting, coaches should remember that they can have more to do with what the coach represents than with anything the coach has done or said. Here, for example, are some common scripts teachers may have running in their minds:

- Since my only observation experiences have been part of formal evaluations, the coach must plan to tell me what I'm doing "right" and what I'm doing "wrong."
- Since we have so many large classes and we could use more teachers, I don't see why the coach isn't teaching classes or pulling small groups each day.
- Since the coach isn't in the classroom, he or she probably doesn't like teaching, so why would I think he or she could help me?
- Since the coach works closely with my administrator or central office, I think he or she is a spy who can't be trusted.

Knowing that teachers may question your motives or skills is a great reason to keep working with the utmost integrity. Showing is as important as telling when it comes to shifting people's thinking about the value of coaching.

Modeling the Way

"We all have two dogs inside of us," writes Jon Gordon (2012). "One dog is positive, happy, optimistic, and hopeful. The other dog is negative, mad, sad, pessimistic, and fearful. These two dogs often fight inside us, but guess who wins the fight? The one you feed the most" (p. 3). When it comes to working in challenging environments, we have to choose between the dogs—not only for our own mental clarity but also for the benefit of the school atmosphere as a whole.

Audrey Goninan, a coach for instructional coaches in South Carolina school districts, encourages her coaches to be positive role models. Her coaches begin all meetings with celebrations, use learning walks to appreciate the strengths in the school, build from strengths when setting goals, and pursue continuous learning through inquiry and learning labs.

Another way to model the way is to collaborate with and strengthen the leadership team at your school. This will take time and will require you to stay the course. When Katrina, a coach in Iowa who wishes to remain anonymous, was faced with a challenging school environment, her first goal was to guide the leadership team. She began by collaborating with the school principal to analyze current data and prioritize an instructional focus area, meeting also with teachers to get their input. It soon became clear that most teachers felt math instruction needed to be improved.

A few members of the leadership team had actually received some training on student-centered math practices that they were excited about and wanted to try. The team as a whole agreed to study these practices in depth before training the elementary staff. Members of the team then partnered with one another to try the strategies out with students. Together the partners would co-plan, co-teach, and co-reflect on the experience, then share results with the leadership team. Team members felt great autonomy and respect in this work.

Coaching Labs

Much as teachers can benefit from the lab sites we discussed earlier, instructional coaches can benefit from participating in coaching labs. Diane Sweeney and her team have been facilitating such labs for more than 15 years, starting with her work in the Denver Public Schools. When Diane came to Iowa to present coaching labs, Kathy had the honor of helping her facilitate them. The groups are usually kept to around 8 to 12 participants. Here is how Diane and Leanna Harris describe the process in *The Essential Guide for Student-Centered Coaching: What Every K-12 Coach and School Leader Needs to Know* (Sweeney & Harris, 2020):

> Coaching labs take us deeper into the practices and decision-making of effective coaching. They are not exemplars of coaching but rather are examples of authentic coaching that stretch thinking. The process involves a prebrief that provides time for the coach to set the focus and share tools and strategies that have been used. Then an observation of coaching is followed by a debrief to unpack implications and points of learning. (p. 123)

The beauty of the coaching lab is that it allows instructional coaches to observe real-time coaching taking place. It is one thing to observe videos or role-play models in the workshop setting, but quite another to see coaching in action.

Coaching Principals

When a school is experiencing dysfunction, coaches are well positioned to help its leaders do something about it. First and foremost, it is critical for coaches to set up ongoing meetings with their school principals—at least 30 minutes each week, if possible. Develop a simple agenda that can provide structure for these meetings. Here's an example Kathy has used that you can adapt to fit your specific needs:

- Review goal from the last meeting. What worked? Each member shares evidence of progress toward the goal. (5 minutes)
- Discuss current challenges. What is the most urgent concern at this time? (5 minutes)
- Discuss possible solutions to challenges. (8 to 10 minutes)
- Discuss next steps. What action steps should be taken before the next meeting? Who will be responsible for what? (10 minutes)

Keysha McIntyre, an educational consultant in Atlanta, Georgia, uses her regular meetings with principals to invite them to embrace coaching. She asks them, "Is there anything you want to know about coaching?" For his part, Ben Owens cites a living mission and vision as key to helping principals embrace a culture of innovation. He often works with them to create an "Image of Possibility"—a vision of what could be possible in their school—and then bringing that vision to life. These discussions bring clarity for the administrator and can magnify their view of how coaching can help.

✳   ✳   ✳

Coaches serve an important role in encouraging healthy school change. Supporting teacher leadership, instituting public teaching activities, building collective efficacy, and making time for celebration are all important goals for using the Compassionate Coaching Focus of Openness to improve schools' professional cultures.

8

Looking Backward, Looking Forward

At the beginning of this book, we all started on a journey. Throughout this journey, we addressed various roadblocks using each Compassionate Coaching Focus. Perhaps individual teachers came to mind as you read, or maybe you saw yourself weaved through the pages. We wrote from the heart, reflecting on our paths as instructional coaches. Honestly, over the almost two years we've spent drafting this book, we have each dealt with many of the barriers discussed in this book, including lack of confidence, overload, isolation, and disruption.

Assessing the Impact of Coaching

Hearing about the impact you've made far down the road is wonderful, but there are actions you can take to formatively assess the effectiveness of your coaching today. Although data related to student achievement or teacher evaluation can be useful, such data is summative and only generated once a year. As Moody (2019) states, "Without formative data that helps us examine the effectiveness [of coaching], we lose valuable time during the school year to ensure the coaching initiative is responsive to the needs of the teachers it supports" (p. 32).

Goal tracking, coaching feedback surveys, anecdotal data, and self-monitoring are just a few of the great formative assessment sources available to coaches. They help us measure what matters most: our day-to-day work with teachers and students. As the late Grant Wiggins (2012) reminds us, "The term feedback is often used to describe all kinds of comments made after the fact, including advice, praise, and evaluation. But none of these are feedback, strictly speaking.... Basically, feedback is information about how we are doing in our efforts to reach a goal" (p. 10). If our goal is to influence teachers' and students' learning, then the way we monitor progress should align.

Goal Tracking

Instructional coaches can keep track of the goals they set at the start of any coaching process with a simple form, such as the one in Figure 8.1.

FIGURE 8.1 Goal Tracker					
Teacher	Goal	Cycle Start Date	Cycle End Date	Was the Goal Met?	Student Evidence

A simple document like this shows goals at a glance and can serve as a reflection tool for coaches. Coaches can also append copies of student work as evidence of goals met. Many schools and districts are looking for ways to report the efficacy of coaching programs to school boards and beyond. The goal tracker, coupled with student artifacts, can be a robust way of communicating progress to stakeholders.

Coaching Feedback Surveys

Having teachers you support respond to statements such as the following on a Likert scale (from "strongly disagree" to "strongly agree") can give you excellent feedback on your impact as a coach. Here are a few of the statements we like to use on our surveys:

- I see the coach as a collaborator rather than an evaluator.
- The coach helps me reflect on my practice.
- I have improved the way I teach based on interactions with the coach.
- I have sustained instructional changes I initiated with the support of the coach.
- I have seen improvement in student learning as a result of my work with the coach.

Surveys might also ask teachers to comment on the strengths of the coach or the coaching program and suggest improvements.

There are a few ways to administer the surveys. Some coaches send them out at specific time intervals, such as every nine weeks; in such cases, intervals need to be long enough for teachers to be able to engage in a coaching cycle or have had some time to reflect on the process. Other coaches only send their surveys out at the end of a coaching cycle. We encourage coaches to send surveys only to teachers they have actually coached; data from teachers with whom they haven't worked will not be useful for improving their coaching.

Anecdotal Notes

Ask the teachers you coach what they found most helpful about the process and jot their answers down. Once you've compiled a good amount of responses, sort and reflect on them. Do you notice any trends? Do the answers align with your views of the coaching cycle? How can you use this information to strengthen your coaching?

Keep in mind that even though this type of data may not yet indicate the effect on student learning, the data can be used by instructional coaches to assess their progress. The key is to reflect on the data to determine what's working and what may need to be revised.

Self-Monitoring

When instructional coach Michelle TeGrootenhuis started monitoring what she did with her coaching time, she soon discovered that the process allowed her to reflect deeply on how to coach with intentionality. Together, she and *her* coach, Kathy, created a Google Sheet to track her time. They listed the various actions Michelle was responsible for, including working within coaching cycles, facilitating professional development, her own professional learning, organizing email, spending time in classrooms, checking/responding to email, and more. They also created pie graphs to visually represent how Michelle spent her time. This process allowed Michelle to be mindful of her time and gave her a way to assess her actions as a coach throughout the school year. She continually reflected on what she was doing and whether it was making an impact.

Please note, this process was her own—not something required. We have encountered coaches who have needed to track all time based on school or district guidelines. Frustration set in when they reported they had no clue what the data was used for.

ACT

We hope these ideas give you some food for thought. As you collect data to measure your impact, set aside some time to reflect along the way—perhaps at the end of each week—using our ACT formula (Perret, 2018a):

- A = What ACTIONS have I completed toward my goals?
- C = What CHANGES have I noticed?
- T = What THINGS do I need to do to get me closer to my desired results?

What's Next?

We've covered quite a bit in this book, and there is no way you can tackle every strategy at once, so we thought we'd provide some suggestions so you can consider a good next step for you. Then consult the section of the book related to your goal to form a plan and regularly consult that section while you work your plan.

- If you are new to coaching or want to refocus your coaching, revisit Chapter 1 for information on how to interact with teachers and get more out of coaching cycles.
- If you have a group of teachers who are encountering a similar barrier, use strategies related to the associated Compassionate Coaching Focus area and its correlating chapter (see Figure 0.1, p. xi) during coaching.
- Use this book as a resource to explore whenever coaching gets difficult.
- Commit to at least one method of formatively assessing the impact of your coaching and reflecting on the assessment data.
- Engage with us! Share how your coaching is going, what has been helpful to you, and what you think we missed on Twitter at @KathyPerret and @kennycmckee. Post your ideas with the hashtag #compassionatecoaching.

✳   ✳   ✳

We want to thank you for taking this journey with us! It is our hope that you have discovered some compassionate coaching strategies to personalize the process and make it more effective.

Over the course of writing this book, our worlds changed both on a personal and worldwide level. A global pandemic broke open the cracks of weak systems, and long overdue racial justice work became a focus for our nation. Through all this time, teachers experienced many of the six barriers discussed in these pages with a high level of intensity. In addition to these events, we each experienced the loss of family members, which led us both to confront many of these barriers ourselves.

We truly understand the power of coaching with compassion at the forefront. We coached each other with compassion and respect to navigate the barriers we experienced so we could help you do the same. We are now even more invested in the power of each Compassionate Coaching Focus area to help teachers improve instruction, and we plan to continue learning about strategies that facilitate a more humanistic approach to the learning of students and teachers.

References

Anderman, L. H., & Leake, V. S. (2005). The ABCs of motivation: An alternative framework for teaching preservice teachers about motivation. *The Clearing House, 78*(5), 192–196.

Anderson, A. R. (2015, November 3). A little appreciation goes a long way: Why gratitude is the gift that keeps on giving [blog post]. Retrieved from *Forbes* at www.forbes.com/sites/amyanderson/2015/11/03/a-little-appreciation-goes-a-long-way-why-gratitude-is-the-gift-that-keeps-on-giving/#51d9f4ce7aaf

Bandura, A. (1994). Self-efficacy. In V. S. Ramachaudran (Ed.), *Encyclopedia of human behavior* (Vol. 4, pp. 71–81). Academic Press; reprinted in H. Friedman (Ed.), *Encyclopedia of mental health* (1998), Academic Press.

Barkley, S. (2016, January 31). Exploring peer coaching [blog post]. Retrieved from *Steve Barkley Ponders Out Loud* at https://barkleypd.com/blog/exploring-peer-coaching

Bolman, L. G., & Deal, T. E. (2010). *Reframing the path to school leadership: A guide for teachers and principals* (2nd ed.). Thousand Oaks, CA: Corwin.

Brown, B. (2018). *Dare to lead: Brave work. Tough conversations. Whole hearts*. New York: Random House.

Brown, B. (2019). *Braving the wilderness: The quest for true belonging and the courage to stand alone*. New York: Random House.

Buckingham, M., & Goodall, A. (2019, March/April). The feedback fallacy. *Harvard Business Review*, 92–101.

Burns, D. (1989). *The feeling good handbook*. New York: HarperCollins.

Calhoun, E. F. (2001). *Every child reads: Accelerating reading achievement through structured school improvement*. Iowa Department of Education.

Covey, S. R. (2016). *The 7 habits of highly effective people: Powerful lessons in personal change*. New York: Free Press.

Craig, P. S. (2010). *Literacy leadership teams: Collaborative leadership for improving and sustaining student achievement.* New York: Eye on Education.

Dam, R. F., & Siang, T. Y. (2020). What is design thinking and why is it so popular? [blog post]. Retrieved from *Interactive Design Foundation* at www.interaction-design.org/literature/article/what-is-design-thinking-and-why-is-it-so-popular

Davis, V. (2016, December 17). Innovate like a turtle [blog post]. Retrieved from *Cool Cat Teacher* at www.coolcatteacher.com/innovate-like-turtle

Deci, E. L., & Ryan, R. M. (2000). Self-determination theory and the facilitation of intrinsic motivation, social development, and well-being. *American Psychologist, 55*(1), 68–78.

Diener, E., & Seligman, M. E. P. (2002). Very happy people. *Psychological Science, 13*(1), 81–84.

Donohoo, J. (2017, October 25). Fostering collective teacher efficacy: Three enabling conditions [blog post]. Retrieved from www.jennidonohoo.com/post/fostering-collective-teacher-efficacy-three-enabling-conditions

Donohoo, J., Hattie, J., & Eells, R. (2018). The power of collective efficacy. *Educational Leadership, 75*(6), 40–44.

DuFour, R., & Eaker, R. (1998). *Professional learning communities at work: Best practices for enhancing student achievement.* Bloomington, IN: Solution Tree.

Durlak, J. A., Weissberg, R. P., Dymnicki, A. B., Taylor, R. D., & Schellinger, K. B. (2011). The impact of enhancing students' social and emotional learning: A meta-analysis of school-based universal interventions. *Child Development, 82*(1), 405–432.

Dweck, C. S. (2007). *Mindset: The new psychology of success.* New York: Ballantine.

Dweck, C. S. (2014, September 12). The power of yet [video]. Retrieved from www.youtube.com/watch?v=J-swZaKN2Ic

Edcamp Foundation. (n.d.). About Edcamp [website]. Retrieved from *Edcamp* at https://digitalpromise.org/edcamp

Edutopia. (2018, August 10). 60-second strategy: Appreciation, apology, aha! [video] Retrieved from www.youtube.com/watch?v=qIel4r3uK9k

Eells, R. (2011). *Meta-analysis of the relationship between collective efficacy and student achievement* [Unpublished doctoral dissertation]. Loyola University of Chicago.

Garmston, R. J., & Wellman, B. M. (2016). *The adaptive school: A sourcebook for developing collaborative groups.* (3rd ed.). Lanham, MD: Rowman & Littlefield.

Gawande, A. (2017, April). *Want to get great at something? Get a coach* [video]. Retrieved from www.ted.com/talks/atul_gawande_want_to_get_great_at_something_get_a_coach

Gazzara, K. (2019, February 20). The difference between coaching and mentoring—and why you need both [blog post]. Retrieved from *Medium* at medium.com/@doctorkevin/the-difference-between-coaching-and-mentoring-and-why-you-need-both-1ab9c894b377

Gordon, J. (2012). *The positive dog: A story about the power of positivity.* New York: Wiley.

Hall, P., & Simeral, A. (2017). *Creating a culture of reflective practice: Building capacity for schoolwide success.* Alexandria, VA: ASCD.

Hattie, J. (2016). Program for the Third Visible Learning Annual Conference: Mindframes and Maximizers, Washington, DC, July 11, 2016.

Holland, K. (2020, June 26). Positive self-talk: How talking to yourself is a good thing [blog post]. Retrieved from *Healthline* at www.healthline.com/health/positive-self-talk

Hurley, M., Kim, S., Srinivasan, M., Hiroshima, C., Bryson, A. M., Meyers, E. J., Kong-Wick, C., & Martinez-Black, T. (2019). *SEL 3 signature practices playbook: A tool that supports systemic SEL: Practical ways to introduce and broaden the use of SEL practices in classrooms, schools, and workplaces.* Oakland Unified School District. Retrieved from schoolguide.casel.org/uploads/2018/12/CASEL_SEL-3-Signature-Practices-Playbook-V3.pdf

Ingersoll, R. M. (2012) Beginning teacher induction: What the data tell us. *Phi Delta Kappan, 93*(8), 47–51.

Jensen, E. (2013). *Engaging students with poverty in mind: Practical strategies for raising achievement.* Alexandria, VA: ASCD.

Johnson, J., Leibowitz, S., & Perret, K. (2017). *The coach approach to school leadership: Leading teachers to higher levels of effectiveness.* Alexandria, VA: ASCD.

Joyce, B., & Showers, B (2002). *Student achievement through staff development.* (3rd ed.). Alexandria, VA: ASCD.

Killion, J. (2019, July). *Coaching roles and responsibilities.* Session presented at the Simply Coaching Summit 2019 [online].

Killion, J., & Harrison, C. (2006). *Taking the lead: New roles for teachers and school-based coaches.* National Staff Development Council. Retrieved from https://learningforward.org/taking-lead-tools

Knight, J. (2007). *Instructional coaching: A partnership approach to improving instruction.* Thousand Oaks, CA: Corwin.

Knight, J. (2016). *Better conversations: Coaching ourselves and each other to be more credible, caring, and connected.* Thousand Oaks, CA: Corwin.

Knight, J. (2018, April 19). The easiest way to triple the impact of coaching: Principal support [blog post]. Retrieved from *Instructional Coaching* at www.instructionalcoaching.com/the-easiest-way-to-triple-the-impact-of-coaching-principal-support

Knight, J. (2019). Why teacher autonomy is central to coaching success. *Educational Leadership, 77*(3), 14–20.

Lewis, S. (2009). *The contribution of elements of teacher collaboration to individual and collective teacher efficacy* [dissertation]. Curry School of Education, University of Virginia.

McKee, K. (2018, January 25). The digital coaching menu: Four reasons why you need one [blog post]. Retrieved from *Aligned* at https://achievethecore.org/aligned/digital-coaching-menu-four-reasons-need-one

McKee, K., & Davis, E. L. (2015, March 17). Watch your language: How to talk so teachers actually listen [blog post]. Retrieved from *SmartBrief Education* at www.smartbrief.com/original/2015/03/watch-your-language-how-talk-so-teachers-actually-listen

Minor, C. (2019). *We got this. Equity, access and the quest to be who our students need us to be.* Portsmouth, NH: Heinemann.

Moody, M. S. (2019). If instructional coaching really works, why isn't it working? *Educational Leadership, 77*(3), 30–35.

Morin, A. (2015, April 3). 7 scientifically proven benefits of gratitude [blog post]. Retrieved from *Psychology Today* at www.psychologytoday.com/us/blog/what-mentally-strong-people-dont-do/201504/7-scientifically-proven-benefits-gratitude

Moss, C. M., & Brookhart, S. M. (2009). *Advancing formative assessment in every classroom: A guide for instructional leaders.* Alexandria, VA: ASCD.

Myers, D. G. (2000). The funds, friends, and faith of happy people. *American Psychologist, 55*(1), 56.

National Board for Professional Teaching Standards. (n.d.). Proposition 4 [website]. Retrieved from http://accomplishedteacher.org/proposition-4

National Council of Teachers of English. (2016, April 10). Professional and personal learning networks [blog post]. Retrieved from *National Council of Teachers of English* at https://ncte.org/blog/2016/04/professional-and-personal-learning-networks

National School Reform Initiative. (n.d.). Critical friends groups purpose and work. Retrieved from www.nsrfharmony.org/wp-content/uploads/2017/10/cfg_purpose_work_0.pdf

Nottingham, J. (2017). *The learning challenge: How to guide your students through the learning pit*. Thousand Oaks, CA: Corwin.

Ostovar-Nameghi, S. A., & Sheikhahmadi, M. (2016). From teacher isolation to teacher collaboration: Theoretical perspectives and empirical findings. *English Language Teaching, 9*(5), 197–205.

Perret, K. (2018a, February 3). A #coachapproach action plan [blog post]. Retrieved from *Kathy Perret Consulting* at www.kathyperret.org/2018/02/03/a-coachapproach-action-plan

Perret, K. (2018b, June 25). The KEYS to coaching conversations [blog post]. Retrieved from *Kathy Perret Consulting* at www.kathyperret.org/2018/06/25/the-keys-to-coaching-conversations

Pumo, M., Korreck, J., Hollis, G., Childers, G., & Zwadyk, B. (2019). Coaching, confidence, and retention: Instructional coaching and new teachers. *CollectivED Working Papers, 9*, 40–47.

Robinson, V., Hohepa, M., & Lloyd, C. (2009). *School leadership and student outcomes: Identifying what works and why*. Best evidence synthesis iteration [BES]. New Zealand Ministry of Education

Saphier, J., & West, L. (2009). How coaches can maximize student learning. *Kappan, 91*(4), 46–50.

Schmoker, M. (1999). *Results: The key to continuous school improvement* (2nd ed.). Alexandria, VA: ASCD.

Stavros, J., Godwin, L., & Cooperrider, D. (2015). Appreciative inquiry: Organizational development and the strengths revolution. In W. J. Rothwell, J. Stavros, & R. L. Sullivan (Eds.), *Practicing organizational development: Leading transformation and change* (4th ed.) (pp. 196–216). Hoboken, NJ: Wiley.

Sweeney, D. (2011). *Student-centered coaching: A guide for K–8 coaches and principals*. Thousand Oaks, CA: Corwin.

Sweeney, D., & Harris, L. S. (2017). *Student-centered coaching: The moves*. Thousand Oaks, CA: Corwin.

Sweeney, D., & Harris, L. S. (2020). *The essential guide for student-centered coaching: What every K–12 coach and school leader needs to know*. Thousand Oaks, CA: Corwin.

Teacher Leadership Exploratory Consortium. (n.d.). *Teacher leader model standards*. Retrieved from www.ets.org/s/education_topics/teaching_quality/pdf/teacher_leader_model_standards.pdf

Togneri, W. (2003) *Beyond islands of excellence: What districts can do to improve instruction and achievement in all schools—A leadership brief.*

Learning First Alliance. Retrieved from https://learningfirst.org/sites/
learningfirst/files/assets/biebrief.pdf

Venables, D. R. (2011). *The practice of authentic PLCs: A guide to effective teacher teams.* Thousand Oaks, CA: Corwin.

Wiggins, G. (2012). Seven keys to effective feedback. *Educational Leadership, 70*(1), 10–16.

Index

The letter *f* following a page locator denotes a figure.

About the Authors

Kathy Perret is an instructional coaching trainer and virtual coach as well as coauthor of *The Coach Approach to School Leadership*. As the founder of Kathy Perret Consulting, she empowers school leaders, instructional coaches, and classroom teachers in their professional growth. With more than 30 years of experience in the field, Kathy hosts onsite and virtual professional learning for educators around the world. Educators directly affect student growth and performance, and Kathy is dedicated to improving experiences and outcomes for both adults and kids. She believes everyone deserves a coach—and that includes teachers, instructional coaches, and school leaders!

Kathy presents at regional, state, and national conferences. She also consults for private and public schools, school districts, state and federal education departments, nonprofits, and educational companies. Besides her work with Kathy Perret Consulting, she serves as a virtual coach for teachers through Sibme and has been an adjunct professor for Morningside College in Sioux City, Iowa. Kathy is the cofounder and comoderator of the #educoach Twitter chat. She has contributed to ASCD Inservice, TeacherCast, and Sibme and has been a popular guest on a variety of podcasts. Kathy can be reached at kathyperretconsulting@gmail.com.

Kenny McKee is a National Board certified teacher who works as a high school literacy and instructional coach for Buncombe County Schools in Asheville, North Carolina. He supports classroom teachers and other school faculty in professional growth and instructional practices. He has 20 years of experience in education as a secondary English language arts teacher and instructional coach. He has also served as a teaching instructor for the department of Literacy, English, and History Education at East Carolina University.

Kenny presents at regional, state, national, and online conferences. He also consults and facilitates professional development for private schools, public schools, school districts, state departments, nonprofits, and education companies. He has contributed writing for Achieve the Core, ASCD, SmartBrief, Virtual Job Shadow, Sibme, TeachThought, and NEA. Kenny can be reached at kennethcmckee@gmail.com.

Related ASCD Resources: Coaching

At the time of publication, the following resources were available (ASCD stock numbers in parentheses).

Building Teachers' Capacity for Success: A Collaborative Approach for Coaches and School Leaders by Pete Hall & Alisa Simeral (#109002)

The Coach Approach to School Leadership: Leading Teachers to Higher Levels of Effectiveness by Jessica Johnson, Shira Leibowitz, & Kathy Perret (#117025)

C.R.A.F.T. Conversations for Teacher Growth: How to Build Bridges and Cultivate Expertise by Sally J. Zepeda, Lakesha Robinson Goff, & Stefanie W. Steele (#120001)

The eCoaching Continuum for Educators: Using Technology to Enrich Professional Development and Improve Student Outcomes by Marcia Rock (#117048)

Educational Coaching: A Partnership for Problem Solving by Cathy A. Toll (#118027)

The Fundamentals of Literacy Coaching by Amy Sandvold & Maelou Baxter (#107084)

Instructional Coaching in Action: An Integrated Approach That Transforms Thinking, Practice, and Schools by Ellen B. Eisenberg, Bruce P. Eisenberg, Elliott A. Medrich, & Ivan Charner (#117028)

The Instructional Playbook: The Missing Link for Translating Research into Practice by Jim Knight, Ann Hoffman, Michelle Harris, & Sharon Thomas (#122020)

Peer Coaching to Enrich Professional Practice, School Culture, and Student Learning by Pam Robbins (#115014)

Personalized Professional Learning: A Job-Embedded Pathway for Elevating Teacher Voice by Allison Rodman (#118028)

For up-to-date information about ASCD resources, go to www.ascd.org. You can search the complete archives of *Educational Leadership* at www.ascd.org/el.

ASCD myTeachSource®

Download resources from a professional learning platform with hundreds of research-based best practices and tools for your classroom at http://myteachsource.ascd.org/

For more information, send an email to member@ascd.org; call 1-800-933-2723 or 703-578-9600; send a fax to 703-575-5400; or write to Information Services, ASCD, 1703 N. Beauregard St., Alexandria, VA 22311-1714 USA.

THE WHOLE CHILD

The ASCD Whole Child approach is an effort to transition from a focus on narrowly defined academic achievement to one that promotes the long-term development and success of all children. Through this approach, ASCD supports educators, families, community members, and policymakers as they move from a vision about educating the whole child to sustainable, collaborative actions.

Compassionate Coaching relates to the **safe** and **supported** tenets. *For more about the ASCD Whole Child approach, visit **www.ascd .org/wholechild**.*

WHOLE CHILD TENETS

1 **HEALTHY**
Each student enters school healthy and learns about and practices a healthy lifestyle.

2 **SAFE**
Each student learns in an environment that is physically and emotionally safe for students and adults.

3 **ENGAGED**
Each student is actively engaged in learning and is connected to the school and broader community.

4 **SUPPORTED**
Each student has access to personalized learning and is supported by qualified, caring adults.

5 **CHALLENGED**
Each student is challenged academically and prepared for success in college or further study and for employment and participation in a global environment.